THE
PEACE
PROMISE

THE
PEACE
PROMISE

TRUSTING GOD TO SOLVE THE UNSOLVABLE

JOHN KUYPERS

BEACON PUBLISHING
North Palm Beach, Florida

Published by Beacon Publishing
All rights reserved.
Formerly titled *The First Rule of Inner Peace: Jesus' Sensible Way to Be Happy*.

Design by Ashley Wirfel

ISBN: 978-1-63582-022-5 (hardcover)
ISBN: 978-1-63582-029-4 (e-book)

Library of Congress Cataloging-in-Publication Data
Names: Kuypers, John, author.
Title: The peace promise : trusting God to solve the unsolvable/ John Kuypers.
Description: North Palm Beach : Beacon Publishing, 2017.
Identifiers: LCCN 2017052416 | ISBN 9781635820225 (hardcover) | ISBN
9781635820287 (softcover) | ISBN 9781635820294 (e-book)
Subjects: LCSH: Peace—Religious aspects—Christianity. | Bible. Matthew, VII,
5—Criticism, interpretation, etc. | Trust in God—Christianity.,
Classification: LCC BT736.4 .K89 2017 | DDC
248.4—dc23

For more information on this title or other books and CDs available through the
Dynamic Catholic Book Program, please visit www.DynamicCatholic.com.

The Dynamic Catholic Institute
5081 Olympic Blvd • Erlanger • Kentucky • 41018
Phone: 1–859–980–7900
E-mail: info@DynamicCatholic.com

First printing, December 2017
Printed in the United States of America

TABLE OF CONTENTS

PART ONE

———◆•◆———

Admit You Lack Peace

ONE

The Peace Promise

Jesus promised us life's greatest reward: "Peace I leave with you; my peace I give you" (John 14:27). But there is a catch. "I do not give to you as the world gives." A friend once said to me, "That's exactly the part that troubles me!" In this book, you will see how radically true that is. It takes courage to receive the peace of the Lord because his ways are not our ways. Only by personal experience will you discover that his ways are also better than our ways.

Jesus encouraged us further by saying, "Let not your hearts be troubled, neither let them be afraid" (John 14:27). Sigh. If only it were that easy.

Consider for a moment what is troubling you. Why does it bother you? Perhaps you feel stuck and unsure what to do. Or you did what you had to do and now you are playing the waiting game; the outcome you want has not happened. Until then, you are not at peace. The finances, the job, the marriage, the children, the divorce, the estranged relationship with your sibling or parent— one of these is stealing your peace.

To reap the peace of Christ, you must face the thief itself: anxiety. Anxiety is an inescapable dilemma that seems unresolvable, not only for you but for all human beings. It is a classic rock and a hard place that leaves you feeling damned if you do and damned if you don't.

Let's look at a peace-robbing situation involving a troubled marriage, in which the ideas of leaving and not leaving both led to a loving wife's deep anxiety.

A reader of one of my previous books, *The Non-Judgmental Christian*, wrote to say she was struggling with how to respond to her husband's infidelity. She wanted to be loving and nonjudgmental, yet every time she forgave him, he would return to and even increase his hurtful ways. She wrote:

> Be it a curse or a blessing, I have a very forgiving heart, and each time I discovered porn sites or communication with someone on a dating site, we would go through the same process: anger that I had been "spying" on him, confession (admittance) of only what I had discovered, declaration that he loved me and didn't want to hurt me, and a promise to never do it again. At first it happened once every six months,

then every three months, until he was going out to local bars and not coming home twice a week.

This wife's unhappy situation illustrates a different dilemma that blocks our path to peace: that of the hammer and the doormat. If she stands up for what she believes, she comes across as if she is wielding a hammer, pressuring her husband to change his ways. If she pushes hard enough, he might change—or he might walk out of their marriage. Yet if she doesn't stand up to his wandering ways, she becomes a doormat, putting up with behavior that is unacceptable to her. Each time she forgave her husband, he acted even more disrespectfully toward her and toward his commitment to her. Indeed, her approach only led him to *increase* the very behavior she did not want. She ended her letter by asking me:

> How can I stay in this marriage and stay nonjudgmental when clearly he continues to make bad decisions that are playing with fire and hurting me so much? I am still crazy in love with this man and he is pretty much a perfect husband with the exception of this deal-breaking behavior.

The dilemma of the hammer and the doormat causes divorces, job terminations, and even wars. Each side wants the other to change. When one refuses, the other either enforces punitive consequences or sweeps the issue under the rug, hoping it goes away by itself. One approach invites immediate conflict, while the other gnaws unhappily at our insides, often for years.

To cope with the angst, we put up thick walls to protect ourselves from criticism or indifference to our needs by those who matter to us. Walls are the reason we fall out of love. They suppress our true thoughts and emotions, eating away at us whether we realize it or not. This ticking time bomb shows up in ill health, cold relationships, and profound unhappiness.

A year later, my reader friend wrote to say she had decided to leave her husband and was at peace with her decision. She had done her best, and that is the most any of us can do. The Bible supports her decision, giving adultery as the only justification for leaving a marriage.

Her life unfolded as it does for many of us. If the people who drive us crazy won't change, we move on. We leave the marriage, quit the job, kick out the adult child still living at home, or find a new best friend. We feel our only other choice is to be treated in ways we find intolerable and unacceptable.

Jesus gave us a powerful escape from this soul-ripping dilemma. It is a path to the promise of his healing, nourishing peace on any given issue. He offered up a teaching about how we can actually cause a change in the person stealing our peace *if* we are first willing to change something in ourselves. I call it the Peace Promise:

"First take the plank out of your own eye and then you will see clearly to remove the speck from your brother's eye." (Matthew 7:5, NIV)

I have been practicing the Peace Promise for more than twenty years. In plain English, this is what it actually means to take the plank from your eye in order to remove the speck from the eye of another:

First get neutral about outcomes, and then you will see clearly what to do.

The plank in our eye blinds us from seeing clearly how to make a right response about outcomes we want from others. As a result, we try and we fail. When we have failed for the umpteenth time, we become utterly convinced that there is no hope. Our spouse will never change. Our job will never get better. Our child will never get on track. Our family of origin will always get under our skin. The plank in our eye becomes petrified wood. We are dead certain that no one can change this person. To think otherwise frightens us. Could we have been wrong for so long?

Jesus said, "Truly, I say to you, whoever says to this mountain, 'Be taken up and cast into the sea,' and does not doubt in his heart, but believes that what he says will come to pass, it will be done for him. Therefore I tell you, whatever you ask in prayer, believe that you have received it, and you will. And whenever you stand praying, forgive, if you have anything against any one, so that your Father also who is in heaven may forgive you your trespasses. (Mark 11:23–25)

My experience is that you will receive what you ask in prayer if you are at peace that you may never receive it. Being at peace first removes your fears and doubts. Now you become capable of believing that you will receive it. Anxiety and doubt are the enemies of deep faith and trust.

Furthermore, you need to forgive and seek forgiveness from those who most upset you—two actions our prideful ego loathes. When we do as Jesus taught, we become instantly neutral. The plank in our eye is gone. We see clearly what the Lord wants us to do. We are at peace if we do not get what we want *and* we can fully expect to receive it. Both of these opposing truths become valid for us. An unknown wise person wrote, "The definition of a genius is someone who can hold two opposing thoughts at the same moment in time." Peace is a paradox.

What would have happened if this wife had stopped trying so hard to save her marriage? What if she had focused instead on becoming neutral about whether her marriage held together or fell apart? What if in so doing, she trusted that God would lead her to wisely respond to her husband's hurtful ways? She would have been a spiritual genius but only in weakness and surrender. For her to do this would have been a leap few of us can make quickly, yet all of us are capable of it.

One reason getting neutral works is that we set others free to make their own choices. Rather than pressuring them to please us or causing them to react defensively against what we want them to do, our unbiased stance causes them to take ownership of their choices and the resulting risks and consequences. They see more clearly the right thing to do when they cannot blame us for their choices.

Setting them free does not mean we offer no opinions! Instead, we couch our opinions with words that make it clear they are free to make their own choices. In so doing, we also set ourselves free to take whatever stand is right for us. This is what unnerves us—to think that we were free all along to respond differently and didn't know it. We often feel trapped in dysfunctional relationships in which the only escape seems hurtful. In reality, the fear of "hurting" someone is often the biggest plank in our eye.

One happy client showed me text messages he received from his wife, apologizing for her cranky attitude that morning. For him, this was a miracle he had wanted for years but had always failed to get. Once he started being calm, centered, and neutral in his response to her moods, she began to change of her own free will. Miracles happen if we are willing to do things Jesus' way. To get them, we must set aside our ego and trust the Spirit within to lead us. This is personal leadership at its highest level. We learn to master our inner self.

Our neutrality builds trust. For relationships with a history of dysfunctional interactions, making this shift can be a turbulent challenge. Long-standing codependencies around deeply ingrained habits need to be broken. But with God, all things are possible, even in the most damaged of relationships. All it takes is two hearts to soften, beginning with your own.

The dilemma of the hammer and the doormat robs us of our peace because we have inner conflict. We want to be true to ourselves. We also want to be accepted by others. The cheated wife faced this inner conflict. She knew that accepting adulterous behavior from her wayward husband was betraying herself. Yet she also feared that if she were too tough with him, he would leave her. She loved him and understandably wanted to save her marriage. In reality, he may have been sabotaging the relationship to get her to be the "bad guy" who initiated the separation—a common and cowardly choice. Thus, her biased desire to save her marriage blinded her from clearly seeing what his true motives were and alternative ways of responding. In the meantime, the bleeding gash in their marriage became deep and irreparable.

Divorce counselor Homer McDonald wrote an intriguing e-book called *Stop Your Divorce*. In it, he advocates living by the principle of neutrality without saying it directly. He says we should act quickly. We should not defend ourselves. We should agree with our divorce-seeking partners that separating is an understandable idea. Agree with their negative feelings about us. Avoid heavy talk. Never act depressed. Remain positive and don't think, "Oh, she'll never change her mind." McDonald points out that because the wife changed her mind about remaining married, she is certainly capable of changing her mind about getting divorced. He understands that setting people free to make their own choices without pressure from us is a powerful way to influence them.

The problem is that if we use these tactics without actually being at peace, we are manipulating people. If the tactic doesn't work, we get upset, proving it was insincere in the first place. We need to have real peace about wrongdoings and negative behaviors we don't like. Having this depth of inner peace requires faith, surrender, forgiveness, and humility. We need to get neutral about what we believe is right. Until we do, we are unable to take wise action, even if it is explicitly pointed out to us. As a coach, I found this to be one of the hardest things to conquer within myself. I needed to get neutral about whether my clients succeeded or failed while still giving them my very best.

Conflict triggers anxiety, and anxiety is the evidence of life's greatest dilemma. German-American theologian Paul Tillich described this dilemma brilliantly in his famous 1952 book, *The Courage to Be*. He outlined how anxiety is caused by the tension between having the courage to "be me" and having the courage to "be-long." If we please ourselves, we risk not fitting in with others and incurring their wrath. If we please others, we risk abandoning our own needs and becoming angry with ourselves. Either way, someone is unhappy. We cannot win; thus, we are always experiencing a certain level of anxiety. Tillich captures a brilliant solution to this relentless struggle: "One could say that the courage to be is the courage to accept oneself as accepted in spite of being unacceptable."[1]

Tillich's conclusion offers us the greatest relief known to mankind. We are imperfect and God loves us anyway, even when other people reject us or when we are mad at ourselves. The life, death, and resurrection of Jesus are the historical proof. Our own practical proof comes from seeing the active presence of the Holy Spirit in our daily life. When we are at peace about the possibility of losing our marriage, failing as a parent, making errors at work, and hundreds of other outcomes we may otherwise fear, we open ourselves to experiencing God's presence in our life. I have had dozens of experiences in which things have worked out in unexpected and beautiful ways when I first let go of trying to control the result I wanted. We do our part and then God does his part. The outcome we get is in his hands, not ours. When this is true for us, the bravest part of our soul is revealed and inner peace is our reward. It is not our job to control the destiny of the universe, let alone what others think of us.

The obstacle to this joy comes when we try to make things right by our own definition. When things don't work out, it is our ego-based nature to want to blame someone and feel unhappy about it along the way. Sometimes we blame ourselves, sometimes others, and sometimes God himself. Ultimately, we always blame ourselves. Even when we think we are not at fault, deep down we accuse ourselves of foolishly trusting the wrong person or being born under the wrong star. We are angry with ourselves, no matter what others have done.

Matthew 7:5 ends this blame game. When we are neutral about outcomes, we stop taking things personally. Paradoxically, we also stop blaming others. Because of this soul-changing spiritual approach, we become reconciled to our own faults and inadequacies. A merciful God loves us anyway. The apostle John described love like this: "There is no fear in love, but perfect love casts out fear" (1 John 4:18).

In order to have peace, we need to drive out fear. Let's explore how Matthew 7:5 spiritually opens our eyes to seeing new ways to resolve old troubles when we first seek his peace.

TWO

How to Recover Your Peace

What did Jesus mean by a "plank" and a "speck"? A plank is a *judgment*. A speck is a *fault*. When we see a fault that bothers us, we judge it because we don't like it. We have a prejudicial view about what we think *should* be happening. Some of our biases are about behaviors, such as dangerous driving, personal hygiene, or angry words. Some biases are based on aspects of the person, such as skin color, accent, gender, or physical deformities. Specks cause us to experience discomfort, upset, and even fear.

Our emotional reaction is the undeniable proof that a nasty speck has entered our presence. My former wife, for example, liked a clean house. She spotted stains like a hawk and smelled odors like a hound dog. These specks drove her crazy. She was attached to an outcome: a clean house. This attachment motivated her to clean messes and get others to be more careful about spills. Since dirt and smells constantly reappeared, she had to be relentlessly vigilant. As long as she didn't mind doing what it took to eradicate stains and smells, she was happy.

This is not so easy when the stains are other people's behaviors. We cannot directly make them be nice, dress properly, behave respectfully, and do what they promised. We have to *get* them to change on their own. We use judgments to do that job for us. Judgments are supposed to eradicate specks. Unconsciously, we hope that when people see that we disapprove of what they're doing, they will change. Sometimes it works and we immediately feel at peace. When it doesn't work, we increase the force of our judgments. We get angry and upset. We inflict punitive consequences. We are trying to remove the speck from their eye, usually with misguided good intentions.

Jesus challenges this habit of ours by saying, "Why do you look at the speck of sawdust in your brother's eye and pay no attention to the plank in your own eye?" (Matthew 7:3, NIV). He questions our approach. He does that right after warning us that our approach will backfire: "Judge not, that you be not judged. For with the judgment you pronounce you will be judged, and the measure you give will be the measure you get" (Matthew 7:1–2).

Luke expressed this same teaching in a slightly different way: "Do not judge, and you will not be judged; condemn not, and you will not be condemned; forgive, and you will be forgiven" (Luke 6:37).

When we judge the faults of others, we have a prejudicial view about what we believe is right and wrong. That bias is the plank in our eye. This is the human way of resolving differences, and it is not sensible. Indeed, it is hurtful and destructive. Does it make sense to respond to someone who yells at you by yelling back? Does it make sense to give the cold shoulder to someone who snubs you? Yet that is exactly what we do.

We get caught in a trap of unhappiness. Our spouse, family, and coworkers keep throwing specks at us. We try to get them to change because their faults upset us. However, our biased view leaks through in the way we respond. We let them know by tone of voice, if not by words. "Do you *mind* letting me know when you're going to be home late?" Our irritation communicates judgmental disapproval. We hope they'll get it and never do it again. All day long, we filter what happens to us through our internal lens of good and bad. Our inner life is a roller coaster of highs and lows caused by how we interpret the way people treat us.

However, we don't always do this. Sometimes, we are naturally neutral and unbiased. A friend asks us out to dinner and wonders what kind of food we prefer. We respond, "I'm easy! Whatever you choose is fine with me.

I'm not a fussy eater." We are indifferent, not in a cold, callous way but in a warm, supportive way. When we show up at the sushi restaurant our friend picked, we are at peace.

On a larger scale, a major purchase such as buying a house forces us to find our point of neutrality. We gauge what the house is worth to us. We make an offer. The seller counters. We counter back. If the price remains too high, we walk away from the deal. Our offer is our stand—our point of indifference. If the seller won't accept it, so be it. We are fine either way, even though some disappointment will accompany the experience. Being neutral doesn't mean being emotionless. Indeed, the effect is quite the opposite. Our emotions test the courage of our convictions. Can we stay true to ourselves or will we fold when we can no longer stand how we feel?

Being neutral helps us see clearly the right thing to do and then do it. People caught up in bidding wars in hot housing markets often live to regret overpaying for their houses. The weight of a large mortgage and the prospect of their house declining in value leave a bad aftertaste. This is what makes this spiritual teaching so practical and sensible. We do the right thing and we have no regrets later on.

The challenge gets much bigger when an outcome is at stake that matters deeply to us. When it is our marriage, parenting, or work life, we have definite views about right and wrong. Those biased views are the plank in our eye. When we practice Matthew 7:5, we are seeking to be neither in favor nor against what they are doing—but only temporarily.

An older man and his thirty-year-old daughter are estranged. She is frustrated by his overbearing and interfering ways. After years of pressing him to back off, she has finally given up. She will not attend family functions when he is present or speak to him in any way. He feels heartbroken. He wants his daughter to know how much he loves her. Instead, she receives his love as a burden too heavy for her to carry. She says she needs to do this to keep her own sanity. He can't seem to adjust to her demands and she can't find a way to get him to stop offering unwanted advice and pressuring her to do things his way. He needs to get neutral about whether she ever speaks to him again. Of course, the same would apply to her if she were the one seeking peace with her father.

A husband and wife fight constantly. Each sees the other as the cause of their problems. She cannot understand why he is so negative. He cannot understand why she is so stubborn. After many years, the pile of specks has grown large. Each can readily rattle off the faults of the other— mean, lazy, thoughtless, selfish, critical, and unwilling to change. Neither sees him- or herself as doing anything materially wrong. One asks, "Is it unreasonable for you to stop getting angry and saying mean things?" The other responds, "Is it unreasonable for you to live up to agreements and stop putting the kids ahead of me?" Each needs to first get neutral about what he or she wants.

Jesus said that if we have a plank in our eye, we will not see clearly how to correct the other's fault. We will fail. The fact that we *are* failing is proof that he is right. Many people choke when I say this. They exclaim, "I have tried everything! Nothing will change this person. Who could possibly put up with what I endure? It's too much!"

However, hidden in the plank is our prideful belief that we can resolve differences with others on our own strength, mostly by trying harder. We do this by putting ever more pressure on them to change. Instead of changing, they dig in and resist more. We get the very opposite of what we want. We are not being sensible. In fact, we are playing God, judging their behavior. The apostle James wrote it this way: "There is one lawgiver and judge, he who is able to save and destroy. But who are you that you judge your neighbor?" (James 4:12).

I coached a senior executive who expressed his frustration with a manager who repeatedly came to him with the problem but never the solution. I asked the executive, "How long has he been doing this?" He replied wryly, "Five years." Rooted in his frustration was his own inability to see a new way to get the behavior change he wanted. Instead, he used the same failed tactic while judging his manager as incompetent in this area of his job. This stood as a personal barrier between them, an obstacle to getting better results from his employee, and a thief of his inner peace. When I suggested we unravel and solve this one, he dismissed it as not worth it. He was unable to see that he could solve the root cause of all his leadership frustrations by exploring this one relationship. He preferred to remain unhappy with his employee. To look closely at the problem would be to face the deeper possibility that he had failed as a leader.

Spouses experience frustration with trying to change each other. My father loves to talk, especially at social gatherings. My poor mother had to fight hard to squeeze a word in. If she complained, he would respond, "I've been this way since you married me, so why are you complaining now after forty years?" He was unwilling to change, and her approach never budged him. Ultimately, she gave up trying, though not without the occasional loud objection.

Many couples find some long-standing habits impossible to accept from their partners. Issues such as emotional distance, a dull sex life, or lack of common interests create a wedge that runs deep and lasts for years. Divorce is often the heart-wrenching solution. Matthew

7:5 offers a hope-inspiring alternative by providing a means to get different results from people who matter to us. If we want to be successful at getting people to meet some of our needs, first we have to remove our biases about how they should behave. Getting neutral is the means to that end.

A client showed me text messages from her husband asking where she was. She said, "He's going to be angry with me when I get home," with a note of dread in her voice. "He hates it when I'm late and dinner isn't made. What should I do?"

I replied, "You should get neutral about whether he is angry or not angry. Then you will see clearly how to respond."

"How do I do that?" she inquired.

"By accepting that he may always be angry with you when you are late."

"Oh," she sighed, her shoulders sagging.

Getting neutral goes against our natural habits. We want to do something that *forces* the result we want right away. We want a magical answer. When we fail, we begin to expect trouble, and more often than not, we get it. Why? Because we didn't take time to get neutral, centered, and unattached to whether we get the outcome we want. As a result, we walk into the room with our defenses up, our counterarguments pre-rationalized, and our escape route planned if things don't go well. Our capacity to listen is low, our heart is hardened, and our stress is high. There is no love in our heart and God is far from our mind.

We can compare getting neutral to shifting gears in a car. Do you recognize these letters every time you drive a car with an automatic transmission?

P R N D

When we want to go forward, we shift into drive (D). If we want to go in the opposite direction, we shift into reverse (R). Without thinking about it, we *temporarily* stop in neutral (N) and prepare the vehicle to change direction by stopping its momentum. If we did not stop and shift into neutral, we would destroy the transmission. The car would keep going in its previous direction despite our desire to go in reverse. Similarly, if we want to change direction in life, we need to stop and *temporarily* shift into neutral. If we don't, our biases make us respond to troubles like a car with only one gear—full steam ahead!

The idea of getting neutral feels unnatural. We think, "What do you mean, get neutral about my boss's bullying? Or my child's misbehavior? Or my spouse's mean-spirited criticism? That would be ridiculous! What they are doing is simply wrong!" When we are convinced that we are right, we do not want to stop and get neutral. We are offended by the other person's stupidity or arrogance, both of which are judgments that blind us. What we are failing to see is that other people have the *right* to make mistakes, even when those mistakes hurt us. All we see are specks that drive us crazy.

One man said to me, "But what if my wife and I have an agreement that I cook four days a week and she cooks three days a week? If I live up to my end of the bargain and she doesn't, am I not justified in being upset with her, especially after repeated requests in a variety of ways?"

I replied, "If you respond while you are upset, you probably have a plank in your eye. If your efforts fail to change her or make things even worse, you can be absolutely certain you are not seeing clearly what to do."

Only after things blow up do we realize that perhaps we made a mistake with the way we responded. Our spouse gets angry with us, our boss fires us, or stress and anxiety consume us and then we finally wake up and realize that failing to seek his peace first only inflames our troubles. Many of us know this intellectually and suppress our feelings, acting cool but not feeling that way inside. Not only does that not work, it makes things worse when the other person realizes we were faking it. This was a major factor in the ending of my first marriage. I was not real with her.

Shifting into neutral is temporary. I cannot repeat this often enough. If we stayed in neutral, we would be stuck and unable to move. Just like with an idling car, stepping on the gas pedal would make the engine roar but the car wouldn't budge. Many of us do this by using empty threats and growling noises but taking no action. Being in neutral is a sacred place and time where we spiritually discern what we need to do to respond wisely to the challenge facing us. It might take minutes or it might take *months* to be at peace with not getting the outcome we want. Once it's done, however, we feel a great relief. We see clearly what we need to do and we are ready to take confident action. This could even mean shifting back into the direction we were already going.

The benefit of first getting neutral is that it opens our mind, heart, and soul to how God wants us to respond. Jesus always teaches us to respond from a place of love. Our subsequent actions may still appear to be biased in the eyes of others, but we are now biased by love, not self-righteous judgment or punitive condemnation. We don't seek to pressure others to agree with us when we are at peace. People notice and they are affected. One example of in-the-moment proof is that they do not get defensive when we speak up. We are respectful even when we are firm and unyielding.

When we are in neutral, we are surrendered. It does not mean we give up our hopes and preferences. It does not mean we stop striving for the outcome we want. However, the stressful struggle of whether we get it is over. The risks and dangers have been digested and accepted. The losses have been mourned. We are at peace with uncertainty and the possibility of things not working out. We respond gracefully in brave new ways.

Chapter three presents two stories of how you can suddenly see new and spiritually insightful ways to get the outcomes you always wanted from others when you first remove that stubborn plank from your own eye.

THREE

Your Soul's Deepest Fear

The practice of Matthew 7:5 begins with noticing within yourself the past moments when something robbed your peace. You have to dig deep in your mind, connecting your unhappy feelings with the exact circumstances when they occurred. Was it how she looked at you? Was it the way he promised you something only to deny it later on? Was it the way she took your honest disclosure and threw it back in your face, making you feel stupid? Was it how someone ignored you, or how you had to explain yourself repeatedly? All you know is that something is off.

We miss the moments that steal our peace because we are not present; we are preoccupied. Our mind is flitting, swirling, and racing from one thought to another. We need to slow down our mind to see what is happening while it is happening. When we are mindful, we see the root of our anxiousness or unhappiness, and how we then do something habitual to numb our feelings such as drink, smoke, or get busily distracted by a shiny object. These unconscious habits blind us.

Being present is not an Eastern spiritual concept, as it is often portrayed. It is merely common sense. Real things happen only in the here and now. Everything else is a memory of the past or a dream of the future. Past and future offer us fears and ecstasies that are not real. Longing for what was or what might be steals our peace now.

Let's take a moment to look at how our mind works in a specific upsetting situation. Something happens. In a heartbeat, we make sense of it. "Is this good for me or bad for me?" The answer we come up with triggers our feelings and influences what we say or do next. Often, we jump to conclusions and make assumptions. Sometimes these are helpful, and sometimes they get us into trouble. Always, they are based on our biased view of the situation, the plank in our eye.

I want you to become aware of how external events flash across your mind, disturb your heart, and threaten your very soul. Noticing how these three parts of your inner self react when you feel triggered is the key to constantly growing your inner peace.

Ken jumps into his car. It is 8:35 a.m. He knows he is barely going to make it to work by nine. He decides to take a back road shortcut. As he drives along, he looks ahead and sees the flashing red signal lights of a railway crossing. "Oh no," he moans. "This will make me late for sure." A flash of frustration rips through his chest as he bangs his fist against the steering wheel. Then his quick mind races through his options. Cut through the protective gates? Pull a U-turn? Take a side street? Call the boss? No option appears better than just waiting it out.

To his chagrin, he sees a slow-moving freight train approaching with three engines resolutely pulling the cars. His heart sinks. This is going to be a long one. His mind flits ahead to the explanation he will soon be offering to his boss as to why he is late once again for the weekly sales meeting. Twenty people will greet his late arrival. Brutal. He can already hear their voices making fun of his habitual tardiness. Ken looks at himself in his rearview mirror. "Why am I such a screwup?" He sinks back into his car seat, feeling anxious and annoyed at his rotten luck. Beating himself up when he makes a mistake is an old and unconscious habit for Ken.

Let's examine what happened. Ken has a biased, prejudicial view about his job: He wants to keep it! On this day, an event occurs that threatens his job security. Although his boss has not actually said or done anything, Ken is aware from experience that he will react with displeasure once he sees Ken has come in late—again.

Here are the thoughts that Ken experienced the moment he saw the train:

1. This train will make me late for work.
2. I need to arrive on time because my boss is expecting it and I agreed to it.
3. My boss and colleagues will think I am unreliable.
4. I could lose my job.
5. I have bills to pay and a family to feed.
6. If I'm penniless, I will be ashamed and homeless.
7. If I'm homeless, I will die.

Points one, two, and three are Ken's mind processing the event and deciding this is bad for him. Points four and five are his heart fearing a potentially painful loss if his boss turns against him and ultimately fires him. Points six and seven are his soul, unconsciously aware of the danger to his very existence. Death is possible.

Strange as it sounds, this is Ken's reality. It is your reality, too. Every time you are happy or unhappy about an event in your life, the internal receptors of your mind, heart, and soul make sense of it, revealing themselves in your body language and tone of voice. Until you are at peace in your soul when facing threatening circumstances, you will experience countless moments of stress and anxiety. How you recover your peace will depend entirely on how you make sense of each situation.

In Ken's situation, he could draw a different conclusion about being late. He could decide that being late does not make him unfit for the job. He could trust that if he loses this job, he will find another and still fulfill his family responsibilities. He could be at peace that if his worst fears come to pass, he will still be a worthy, lovable human being. This level of trust requires Ken to admit that he does not control his future. This is what is most unsettling about Jesus' teaching. Trusting the future to God without worrying and fretting is a foreign experience for most of us. But when we do, we feel the great relief that comes with having faith in something bigger than ourselves. A faith-filled friend once assured me, "We don't know what the future holds, but we know who holds the future!"

Without this assurance, we have anxious thoughts for one main reason: to protect ourselves. We have a voice in our head that I have named "Protector," a voice that analyzes what is happening, preplans what to say and do, and criticizes when we mess up. We need to make friends with this voice. It often seems negative and is sometimes known as our "inner critic." It is actually protecting our ego—from our real self. Protector believes that our real self is dangerous and cannot be trusted. Our real self might say or do something stupid like criticize our boss, say something embarrassing, or have an impulsive sexual fling. Sometimes, this real self is characterized as our "inner child"—emotional and immature.

Protector is a filter that presents an improved version of who we are to the people around us. In so doing, it actually robs us of our peace. We are double-minded. One part of us knows our real truth. Another part of us formulates what we think we need to say to be accepted and approved of by people who matter to us. This is what makes us hypocrites, and it produces anxiety.

The apostle James described what a person who is experiencing doubts is like: "Such a person is double-minded and unstable in all they do" (James 1:8, NIV). When the plank is out of our eye—that is, when we have removed our judgments about the situation—we are relieved of anxiety and self-doubt. We are at peace because we first became neutral about outcomes before we acted. We accepted that what happens next is not in our control. There is nothing to self-doubt or second-guess. We don't even pray that things will go our way. Instead, we pray, "Thy will be done."

To successfully practice Matthew 7:5, you need to overcome the emotion-based Protector and develop a trust in your spirit-based self—your soul. As you do, you will cultivate a compassionate inner voice, one that supports you when you make mistakes that cause you to lose things you value, such as your marriage, job, or money. The critical inner voice that plays like a negative recording in your mind begins to fade away, one judgmental plank at a time.

You will find a large measure of peace when you are single-minded, not double-minded. The key is to have nothing to hide. A common phrase for this is to "be authentic" or "be real." My reliance on Protector meant I could not see my own true motives until I stopped hiding my true thoughts and feelings. When I became real with others, I became real with myself. Jesus starkly described what we are doing to ourselves spiritually when we hide our darkest secrets:

> This is the judgment, that the light has come into the world, and men loved darkness rather than light because their deeds were evil. For everyone who does evil hates the light, and does not come to the light, lest his deeds should be exposed. But he who does what is true comes to the light, that it may be clearly seen that his deeds have been wrought in God. (John 3:19–21)

Having nothing to hide is a vital ingredient in becoming neutral about issues that trouble us. Being real empowers us and is the most effective way I know of to build self-confidence. We are affirming to ourselves that we are worthy. We are choosing not to abandon ourselves in order to please or impress others. Instead, we are growing our capacity to feel safe and secure within, even when others are unhappy with us. Early in our journey, however, we need a safe, confidential place to expose our dark side to the light. I found such a place early in my journey, and there under God's loving light, I looked squarely at the most peace-robbing relationship of my life—with my father.

My father was a hardworking Dutch farmer who came to Canada at age twenty-four, right after he and my mother married. His focus on working long, hard hours meant he spent very little time with me. As I grew up, he never attended a sports game of mine or a parent-teacher night. As far as I could tell, he put little effort into knowing what I was doing other than tracking whether I was doing my farm chores. Even then, he left it up to my mother to play the heavy and get me into the barn each night. As a result, I had a distant relationship with him. Deep down, however, I craved more, so much so that I actually quit my corporate job at twenty-five and started a carrot farm near his farm, which lasted one year. When that didn't work out, I returned to the corporate world, which further distanced me from him for several years, making our relationship tense and uncomfortable.

I was early in the second year of learning about being present, vulnerable, and nonjudgmental when an unexpected moment occurred. I opened myself to expressing my real feelings about my relationship with him in a safe place. I was no longer able to pretend that I didn't need anything from my dad.

I was taking a full-time personal growth course that lasted eight weeks. In the fifth week, I admitted to the class that I wanted much more than a superficial relationship with my father. My instructor helped me see that my biased views of my father were preventing me from seeing what I needed to do to truly change my relationship with him.

Here is how the instructor did it. He asked me to do a role-play with the class, in which I would say aloud exactly what I wanted from my dad, just as if he were sitting in the room. Though puzzled by his plan, I agreed to it because I trusted him.

I began tentatively, "Dad, I want a meaningful relationship with you where we talk about how we feel and not just the weather."

The entire class suddenly responded in unison, "Not interested!" I was stunned. I had no idea how the leader had coaxed the class to do this, but before I could start analyzing, he again urged me to say what I wanted.

I gathered myself and said, "Dad, I want a meaningful relationship with you where we talk about how we feel and not just the weather."

Instantly, the class responded loudly, *"Not interested!"*

My head reeled. My instructor urged me on. "Say what you want one more time." I took a deep, determined breath. "Dad, I want a meaningful relationship with you where we talk about how we feel and not just the weather."

"NOT INTERESTED!" boomed the class.

The roar of their words crashed through whatever pretense of civility I had maintained. I boiled with rage. My instructor gazed at my furious face and patiently asked, "What's coming up for you?"

"What's coming up for me is a great big f--- you!" The words seared off my tongue like a hot branding iron.

"Why is that?" he asked, unfazed.

"Because if you reject me, I'll reject you!" I snarled.

He gazed back in a quizzical, nonjudgmental way. "Does that get you what you want?"

My chest collapsed like the last gasp of a deflating balloon. After a long pause, I said, "No, it doesn't. . . ." My voice trailed off. The impact penetrated my very soul.

Instantly, I became aware of the plank in my eye. I realized that by blaming my father for the state of our shallow relationship, I had been excusing myself from taking responsibility for my own role in this unhappy state of affairs. I immediately became conscious of my long-held belief that he had to make the first move. My bias was gone. I was finally neutral. That awareness gave me the courage to take action. My instructor suggested that I call my father and tell him what I really wanted. I responded in a determined voice, "I can do better than that. I'm going home this weekend and I will tell him in person."

That weekend I faced my greatest fear: confronting my father with my real feelings in an open and vulnerable way. Twice that weekend, I summoned my courage only to fall away trembling, unable to face my deep fear that he might reject me. All I could imagine was his voice responding with pity and disgust, "You weak little boy."

In desperation, I finally wrote him a letter on Sunday morning. I bravely handed it to him in his living room, right after he came home from church with my mother. I waited, my heart pounding, while he read it. My mother stood by, holding her breath in anticipation.

In the letter, I thanked him for the good things I had received from him. Indeed, they were far more plentiful than I had ever given him credit for. Most poignant was what I did not write. I made no mention of any of his faults. Furthermore, I took responsibility for my own failings and shortcomings. I ended the note by asking him to speak up now if anything I had done over the years bothered him in any way.

When he finished reading it, he burst into tears. How I respected that. I hadn't shed a sobbing tear since I was thirteen, and I knew it was a towering barrier to my own desire for inner peace and serenity. To my amazement, he cried because I had not called him two months earlier, right after he'd had surgery. I stood up, apologized for failing him, and, along with my mother, we hugged. In that moment, we buried the past forever.

He and I now have an open, loving, and supportive relationship that is going on eighteen years. I consider it my greatest achievement, though I did not do it on my own strength. I lived out Matthew 7:5, driven by my desire for peace and supported by a wise coach who threw my biggest fear directly in my face. God opened my eyes to see a new way to get what I wanted.

Surprisingly, I never needed to hear an apology from my dad in return. This later became a major platform in my coaching and workshops that I call "Reverse Forgiveness." It is living out the golden rule in Luke 6:31: "Do to others as you would have them do to you." When I gave my father what I'd wanted him to give to me—a heartfelt apology for past wrongs—the Holy Spirit gave me the healing I wanted, without my needing anything from my dad. This is one of the greatest spiritual mysteries I have ever encountered. Consider doing this in your situation. In your heart of hearts, what do you wish the other person would give you? Give that very gift to him or her, without expecting anything in return.

Having coached many people in their quest to solve difficult personal and leadership issues, I believe that to truly experience lasting peace, particularly in your marriage, you must come to a place of complete forgiveness and compassion for your parents. I am aware that for some people this can seem like an insurmountable barrier. Yet if you become neutral about the way your parent(s) treated you, you will see clearly how to heal past wounds, end present frustrations, and be at peace with the man or woman who brought you into life. You cannot know until you do it, even if you have tried dozens of times in the past. You must overcome the paralyzing and false belief that your past equals your future.

An excellent way to begin being real is to keep a private journal. In it, note events that upset you, how you responded, and whether you had the full picture of what was going on. Being real begins with being brutally honest with yourself. Later, you must become willing for others to see your truth. To not do so is to remain imprisoned in fear of what other people think of you. It is nerve-racking to do this at first. For this reason, you need one of four motives to get committed to taking the first step to seeking his peace, *and* you must avoid the one motive that never works.

PART TWO

---◆◆---

Get Committed

FOUR

Four Ways to Get Committed

Before I began my spiritual journey, I was a "self-improver." Learning was my happy place. I read books and took courses with a voracious appetite, in constant search of building a better (and happier) me. I stumbled across the book *Flow*, by Mihaly Csikszentmihalyi. A professor at the University of Chicago at the time, he was curious to understand what made people happy. He did a massive research project in which he equipped several thousand people with pagers in the pre-Internet, pre–cell phone days of the 1980s. He buzzed his participants eight times a day for a week, asking them to write down what they were doing and how they were feeling in that moment. He and his research team then analyzed more than one hundred thousand such experiences, conducting interviews as well.

What Dr. Csikszentmihalyi found became a fork in the road for me. He proclaimed that truly happy people are intrinsically happy, regardless of their external circumstances. I instinctively knew the professor was right. I also knew I did not possess this mysterious and vaunted gift. Neither did 50 percent of the population, according to his research. The rest of us weaklings depended on extrinsic factors for our happiness; our outward circumstances defined our inner experience.

I eagerly read *Flow* to the very last page, hoping Csikszentmihalyi would reveal the recipe for intrinsic happiness. Disappointingly, he gave no answer. Instead, he drew this philosophical conclusion: "People who learn to control inner experience will be able to determine the quality of their lives, which is as close as any of us can come to being happy."[2]

I was puzzled by two examples he gave of people who were intrinsically happy. One was an old woman who was a dairy farmer in the Italian Alps. Each day, Serafina repeated the same routine, leading her cows high into the mountains after the morning milking, then returning each evening for the second milking of the day. She loved the path, the flowers, the birds, and her village. The second example was an Egyptian man who decided to spend twenty years walking around the eastern end of the Mediterranean Sea from Egypt to Italy with nothing but the clothes on his back. Each morning, Reyad wondered how he would find food that day. Each night, he wondered where he would sleep, from ditches to bridges to the homes of total strangers who offered unexpected hospitality. He started his journey at age thirteen. At thirty-three, he summed up his life experience like this: "To be a man means to be responsible, to know when it is time to speak, to know what has to be said, to know when one must stay silent." Reyad had learned to trust his inner self.

The contrast between these two experiences made no sense in my analytical and self-absorbed brain. One person lived in what I considered to be a mind-numbing daily routine, one I had known with distaste as a farm boy. The other lived in total poverty and uncertainty, with seemingly no purpose or direction in life. How could both of these extremes lead to the same deep sense of inner peace and intrinsic happiness? I was left with only one clue to this mystery: The professor observed that having too many choices makes us unhappy and that people with limited choices are the happiest. What an unappealing thought. I sighed, wringing my hands in frustration.

Five years later, the seed of the answer fell into my lap. Oh, I had been looking hard already. Over those five years, I suffered a stress-related and shocking blackout on the family room floor. It was God's wake-up call, which became the defining moment of my adult life. A year later,

I quit my corporate job for good and became a strategy and organizational change consultant. I changed my diet and lost weight. I saw a stress counselor for three months. I began meditating daily. I increased my exercise program. All helped but none worked. I still felt an unease within that incessantly nagged. I simply could not see what was bothering me or what I could do about it.

In a commuter train parking lot on a gray November day, a colleague mentioned that he and his wife had found an amazing solution to their young son's autism. It was a program that taught parents how to "be in the present." I will never forget the look of joy and hope on this father's face. He explained that being present meant totally accepting their child's behavior without any desire or attempt to change it. "If the child spins a plate, you spin a plate. If the child makes strange noises, you make strange noises." The goal was to make the child feel so loved that he would want to emotionally reconnect with his parents of his own free will, without pressure or behavior modification. All these aching parents wanted were a few seconds of recognition and eye contact.

For reasons known only to a God I had long ago rejected, this message struck me like a bolt of lightning. I instantly recognized that I was never in the present. My mind was constantly and relentlessly chewing on the future while analyzing past events, looking for cause-

and-effect relationships in order to make decisions that would lead to a better, happier future. I saw with shocking clarity that I traveled on a commuter train every day with thousands of other people and never noticed even one of them. They were amorphous blobs taking up space while I busily solved an endless stream of problems in my head. For the first time, I saw that I was never content with my present situation. Much later, I realized that this meant I had shut love out of my life. My inability to love was the root cause of my lack of peace. I had no idea how deep this well needed to be drilled. I was aware only that I felt empty inside and I wanted to fill my lifelong emptiness more than anything else in the world.

This awareness motivated me to begin a pursuit for inner peace that has carried me for more than twenty years. If you want to experience the spiritual healing of constantly growing peace, you need to begin with an unshakable motive. There are four ways God will use to wake you up to the kind of commitment you need to successfully master the Peace Promise. Importantly, there is a fifth one that does not work.

These are the four motives God uses:

1. **You need a new kind of hope brought on by a personal calamity.** This is typically the heartbreak of a divorce, death of a loved one, serious illness or

injury, financial crash, and so forth. Unhappiness and depression are often the consequences.

2. **You need peace in a relationship filled with relentless emotional pain.** He or she is driving you crazy and you cannot bury your pain any longer. Often it is with a spouse, parent, in-law, or child. It could be with a neighbor, ex-spouse, or colleague at work. Caregivers are often in this group.

3. **You need a new purpose for your life.** This is usually caused by external success accompanied by the shocking realization that when your dreams come true, you are still chronically unhappy. Athletes, actors, and businesspeople come to mind. This was a big part of my original motive.

4. **You need to operate at your peak performance.** Being centered, clear, and calm is vital to your performance success as a coach, pastor, leader, therapist, or stage performer.

The perceived need for self-improvement is the fifth motive, and it does *not* lead to the commitment you need. Self-improvers (like me at one time) are intellectually interested in personal growth but are unwilling to take the real-world risks that come with making authentic changes. If you are satisfied with the status quo in your life, this book will make an interesting read but little more.

Valerie from California was ready to practice Jesus' ancient, wise teaching. She described to me how she changed as a person after regularly practicing Matthew 7:5:

> My biggest behavior change is in my mouth. Who has noticed? Every single person who knows me and who knew me before. One of my sisters said to me, "I've always loved you but I didn't like you. Now I love you and like you!" People have noticed and commented that I don't seem angry all the time. I no longer feel the need to say everything I think, and my relationship with my husband is much more enjoyable. I don't confront him on things the way I used to.
>
> My eyes were opened to a new way of seeing, my ears were opened to a new way of hearing, and I am a new person. I don't mean to exaggerate, but this is true. I don't mean to give the impression that I don't ever say the difficult things—because I do. However, my approach is different. My focus isn't on being "nice." Rather, I strive for authentic, and I don't rush into comments. I take a moment and focus my thoughts before speaking, at least most of the time.

I was deeply moved by Valerie's note—her sincerity and the scope of the changes she experienced. What had really changed for her? Her attitude. Applying Matthew 7:5 before we act moves us from the human attitude toward Jesus' attitude. We choose words that touch others in a deep and real way. Previously tense situations become easy moments that we resolve with confidence and patience.

Attaining a high level of peace comes at a cost. Just look at what the apostles and saints gave up in order to have the peace of Christ. I want you to understand that I paid a high price in time and money to learn the tools I describe in this book. This is without factoring in the life-changing events that God uses to teach us how to lean on him. You need to consider the ways in which you are holding back your wallet and your time. Jesus demands everything we have.

I invested $12,000 in ten weeks of full-time personal growth and coaching courses. I spent $8,000 on one-on-one therapy, and an additional $5,000 attending a weekly men's therapy group over two and a half years. I left my first marriage, learned huge lessons in family court, dated several women while single again, changed careers, cut my work time and income drastically, read more than thirty books, and became a Christian. Subsequently, I wrote books, spoke to audiences, and taught workshops. Even with all that, I had deeper wounds yet to heal, which came about in my second marriage.

This was my spiritual journey. Yours might look vastly different. The Peace Promise is a spiritual tool you can rely on time and time again to help you see clearly what you need to do and trust the outcomes to him. However, the cost, in terms of both time and money, is not free.

Many people have found a satisfying level of peace by merely practicing Matthew 7:5 with a focus on "peace first, results second." They commit to putting his peace ahead of being right—about money, sex, the right way to raise a child, losing weight, the best church to belong to, and a myriad of other outcomes to which they were previously heavily attached. Every day offers new opportunities to those who seek his peace above all else.

Your path to peace will be uniquely yours. Furthermore, if God wants you to learn a lesson on how to lean on him, I don't believe you will successfully avoid it. If you face repetitive struggles, you can be sure God is knocking on your door, urging you to trust him by no longer relying solely on your own strength. Our journey closer to God never ends, but his peace is rich and bottomless. Jesus described the journey like this: "The kingdom of heaven is like treasure hidden in a field, which a man found and covered up; then in his joy he goes and sells all he has and buys that field" (Matthew 13:44).

We are constantly challenged to "sell" what we own— that is, to become detached from outcomes we value in order to "buy" the treasure that is God's lasting peace. Practically speaking, this is a daily process of grieving lost hopes and dreams followed by the quenching spiritual relief and growing trust that his love and his ways are better than the plans we had in the first place. Jesus said, "Blessed are those who mourn, for they shall be comforted" (Matthew 5:4). Removing each plank involves a loss that feels painful at first but sets you free afterward.

Practicing the Peace Promise will change many things in your life, like how you raise your children. A Christian mother of four had her eighteen-year-old, eldest daughter living at home while she attended her first year of university. Mom's problem was that the daughter often came home late and woke up the entire household. When Mom complained, daughter knowingly replied, "Fine, I'll just move out." Some parents might say, "Fine, let me help you!" But this mom was heavily attached to keeping her daughter at home. To be at peace and to solve this problem, Mom needed to become neutral about where her daughter lived. I explained this spiritual possibility to her, whereupon she promptly replied, "Well, I guess I'll live with my daughter's noise." For her, Matthew 7:5 served its purpose in a different way. She did not want to change and so made no effort to first get neutral. Instead, she accepted the outcome that originally upset her so much.

As a parent, I sometimes felt the dangerous allure of being baited by my son when he was a teenager and he complained about things I asked him to do. I constantly reminded myself, "Don't bite the hook. He is doing the task and that's what matters." When he was done, I complimented him. Ignoring unwanted behavior and rewarding good behavior becomes easier when we first get neutral about people whose complaints grate at us. We respond differently and they are affected by it. This solves an extremely common leadership error I see in clients. These leaders reward bad behavior with lots of attention and ignore good behavior, taking it for granted. This bad leadership habit makes no sense at all when you think about it!

You have to change how you handle adversity if you want the peace of Christ all day, every day. When you use the Peace Promise, you focus on what people do, not what they say. For those going through the agony of a divorce battle, I advise them, "Watch only what the other person does, not what he or she says."

Judgmental words are used to inflame us. People are also deceived by flattery and false praise. Either can draw us into doing things we later regret. Superficial friends speak empty words that sound good in the moment: "Hey, I'll call you." "I'll have you over for dinner sometime." "I'll look after that for you." When they don't deliver, we know they fell into the trap of wanting to please without counting the cost. I love the ancient proverb, "Wounds from a friend can be trusted, but the enemy multiplies kisses" (Proverbs 27:6, NIV). A true friend is honest, even if he or she hurts your feelings. An enemy tells you what you want to hear. You need to begin by being a true friend yourself. Otherwise, when you are found out, people will be angry with you. Better is immediate anger that is authentic than delayed anger that is ignited by your falsely kind words.

Many people would rather keep their biased views and wallow in the unhappiness of long-standing problems. Some are addicted to the drama and the attention it gets them. Looking for sympathy, they love to tell one-sided "poor me" tales of how they are being victimized. Often they do things that bring on the very oppression they complain about, trapped in a destructive cycle of judgmental attacks and counterattacks. Others push people away to avoid attention. They hate conflict and want to keep things on the surface at any cost. They feel alone and isolated yet do things that penalize anyone who would dare rock their boat.

In both approaches, unhappiness is a dysfunctional way to avoid taking bold action to resolve troubling issues. They use unhappiness to justify standing pat while pointing out how the other person needs to change. I lived like this for too many years, paralyzed by inaction. I needed one of the four motives to get committed to seeking what my heart yearned for: the life-giving peace of Christ, who heals all wounds and fills the hearts of those who believe in him. I needed to realize that when all my dreams came true, I was still empty on the inside without his love.

You can enjoy his peace and love, just as Jesus promised: "He who loves me will be loved by my Father, and I will love him and manifest myself to him" (John 14:21). God will show himself to you through the results you get if you first let go of your own idea of the right and wrong way to do things.

Let's see how your bias toward thinking you are right in any struggle with another person is actually your biggest obstacle to seeing clearly what you need to do to both solve the issue and be at peace.

FIVE

Why You Can't See Clearly

Sandra is fifty-two years old and is a successful professional. For the past five years, she has battled her ex-husband over money matters. Along the way, she has dated men using online dating services. None have worked out. The experience of putting herself out there, getting her hopes up, and then being rejected over and over again has slowly crushed her self-esteem. She is ready to give up on her dream of having someone in her life with whom to grow old. She is even ready to give up on God, feeling he doesn't hear her prayers.

George is forty-three years old and owns a profitable, growing business. His brilliant innovations have made his company the leading vendor in his industry. Every time his company develops a new product, however, he ends up being the project manager. He is frustrated that the well-paid professionals he has hired somehow drop the ball when launching new products. The stress is beginning to take a toll on his health; it's such a normal part of his daily life that he no longer knows what inner peace feels like.

Sue has been married for twelve years and has three children. Her husband is a high-profile professional, well-respected in the community. Privately, however, he is needy and controlling. He wants her to greet him at the door with eager arms and wearing a negligee. She tries to please him but nothing ever quite lives up to his relentless fantasy of the perfect Christian wife. They are fighting more than ever and she worries that she is getting depressed. She is at the breaking point and seriously wants to leave him. He is no longer the kindhearted man she once knew. Rather, he is smothering and demanding. She feels angry, guilty, and in despair.

Josh is twenty-four years old and single. He has a good job in the IT field. He is a gamer, often playing online video games for three hours a day. Sometimes he spends time at his parents' cottage, where there is no Internet. There, he finds himself easily bored. He drinks several beers to quell the angst. Sometimes he smokes marijuana with his friends. He finds dope calming.

Frustration, despair, loneliness, and boredom are powerful signs that we are unhappy. Something is not right. We are not getting the outcomes we want. Sandra wants to meet a new mate. George wants his business to run smoothly. Sue just wants to be loved as she is, not as a sexual fantasy. Josh doesn't know what he wants. He is still figuring out his place in the world, where choices are plentiful and happiness is a constantly moving target.

George rationalized his need for control this way: "I don't want control. I just want things to be *in* control." As if one is not the same as the other. We loathe uncertainty. We want outcomes we cherish to unfold the right way—our way. I had this need, too. When I was thirty-four years old, I was vice president of a large food and beverage company, eager to rescue a hurting business in a tough economy. My happiness was tightly linked to doing a good job and constantly building my career. One day after returning home from a stressful business-vacation trip to Europe, I got up from the couch and suddenly blacked out for a few seconds, slumping to the family room floor like a sack of potatoes. My wife helped me stagger up the stairs to bed, where, eighteen hours later, I had the sobering realization that my health was in serious danger. I could die. God had hit me between the eyes with a two-by-four. I became convicted that something real needed to change in my life, though I had no idea yet what that should be. I only knew that my idea of what was the "right" way to live my life had failed me miserably.

When we arrive at that shuddering moment of awareness that we are not at peace, we realize that we are
responsible for finding it. No one else can give us peace.
Our only choices are to do something about it or continue
to suffer, either in silence or with griping complaints.

American evangelist Billy Graham's daughter Anne
Graham Lotz discovered later in life that doing things
Jesus' upside-down way brought her lasting peace, but
she struggled with how to do it. She published a book,
Wounded by God's People, acknowledging how often she
felt hurt by other Christians. At the age of sixty-five, she
discovered the stunning impact of Matthew 7:5 in her
own life. She described how failing to follow this teaching
robs us of our peace:

> When you and I focus on the speck of sin in the other person's
> life while paying no attention to the plank in our own, God
> will begin to get our attention. He may use a lack of peace,
> an absence of joy, an agitation of spirit, a knot in the pit of
> our stomachs, a dullness or depression in our emotions or
> something else to alert us that we are not all right.[3]

Ms. Graham Lotz called these "spiritual blind spots."
After describing how a friend refused to forgive her and
then bluntly and permanently severed their relationship,
she became more committed to applying Jesus' teaching to

see more clearly what she needed to do. She was surprised at how challenging it was:

> In spite of the fact that I want to "see," I've found it difficult, if not impossible, to open my own eyes. I know I have blind spots but I just can't see them.[4]

A major reason we can't see our blind spots is because there are two perspectives in every situation. One spouse's adultery is the other spouse's finding of a soul mate. One person getting the job done well is another person feeling pushed and criticized as not good enough. When my son was seven years old, I was pitching him a baseball and he kept missing. Finally in frustration, he exclaimed, "Dad! You're pitching the ball too high!" That was what he saw. I saw that he was swinging the bat too low. These two valid "truths" were happening at the same moment in time!

We feel wounded—and blinded—by the perspective that affects us. We feel pain because our sense of right and wrong has been violated. We want to make things right, if we can. The problem is, what is right? Is a clean sink right? Is making love every day right? Is it right to expect restitution from the person who hurt us?

Right is in the eye of the beholder. When things are right—as we see them—we are at peace. When they are not, neither are we. However, our version of right is a relative truth, not an absolute one. For example, some women walk bare-breasted in public to protest the lack of women's rights. Others walk in public cloaked in a burka, with no part of their body visible, including their eyes. Many people feel pressured to dress according to the latest fashion trends. What is the right way to dress? We know only that we feel ill at ease if we are dressed inappropriately.

Each of us has our own definition of what is right. For most of us, that code is unwritten and unconscious. We are aware of our feelings; we know something has upset us. It could be a small event such as ordering a coffee with cream and sugar only to find out they forgot to put in the sugar. It could be a major disturbance such as trouble at work, a rebellious child, or a major health setback. Whatever it is, we experience our loss of peace as mental stress, emotional anguish, and a physical drain. When we are at peace, we feel the opposite. Our mind is clear, our emotions are calm, and our body is relaxed.

Perhaps you have forgotten how it feels to be centered and at peace. I was first shocked into this awareness when I was twenty-four. After working in a fast-paced corporate marketing job for two years and loving it, I took a three-week vacation across Europe with my best friend. During my travels, I became conscious of how deeply relaxed I felt. The absence of tension was a revelation. I was alarmed to realize that I had been living in a constant state of stress. I then made four career moves in twenty-three months in the futile hope of resolving my inner tension. None worked. I had not yet learned that the cure for tension, stress, and anxiety lay within me, not in a different job. Furthermore, I still believed that I needed pressure and deadlines in order to perform at peak levels.

Life reinforced these beliefs. At work, each new boss praised my performance and then pointed out "areas for improvement." One boss warned me, "Your life will never be simpler than it is today." It was his ominous alert that the burden of leadership constantly grows. At home, my first wife spotted my deficiencies—the times I forgot to do what I said I would do, failed to clean up, or acted in ways that were hurtful or disappointing to her. My parents had done the same as I grew up on the family farm, pointing out my shortcomings ranging from not doing chores properly to secretly smoking cigarettes. The message I received from all these well-intentioned fault finders was the same: *You are not good enough as you are now. You need to be aware, be worried, and push yourself if you are going to make the grade and be successful.* In the school of life, we learn it is results that count. We need to meet or exceed expectations. Sometimes, this drives us to become perfectionists who are hard on others and on ourselves.

Two barriers to your peace are hidden in this old and common pattern. One is that you are at peace only when you achieve a desired result. You learned that results come first and peace comes second. You also learned that other people determine what those results need to be. Someone else decides how clean the sink needs to be, how clean the house needs to be, what a quality job looks like, and whether you are worth loving or dumping.

We fall into the trap of letting our peace depend on other people and their definition of what is right. When they are mad at us, we feel bad about ourselves or angry at them. Of course, we do the same to them. We let them know when we are unhappy with their performance. They react, whether they thank us for pointing out their deficiencies, ignore us, or counterattack with a volley of defensive accusations. Hidden from our sight is a tense boundary battle, each of us trying to make the other do things the "right" way.

I feel sad at how often I meet committed Christians who follow Jesus but do not have the peace he offers. Their hearts are troubled and their unhappiness is marked by anger or false bravado. One devout woman, let's call her Amanda, complained that a Christian organization to which she has belonged for many years is changing. The membership is shrinking. The new leader is too inexperienced for the job. The old leader moved on too soon. The people running the highest levels in the organization are doing it wrong and don't listen.

Some members don't even show up at pro-life events. Amanda says she is no longer being "fed" and has stopped attending most events. Underneath is an unhappy person who wants things to be done the right way—her way.

Many of us get discouraged with groups and organizations we belong to. We are not at peace, and at some level we blame the group. We don't feel appreciated for our hard work and dedication. We then swing the other way, unhappily withdrawing while withering under a critical spirit.

Wherever you are in your life journey, you will never experience lasting peace until you come to terms with how other people affect you. People wounded you when you were young. They wounded you when you were older. You wounded them, too. We did it to each other by trying to get what we wanted from one another. We wanted sex and sometimes we manipulated someone to get it. We wanted attention and sometimes we lashed out to get it. We wanted to be left alone and sometimes we abandoned people we cared about to avoid dealing with complicated problems.

Some people of faith think all they need is God in order to have his peace. But Jesus never offered this as an option. He said the two greatest commandments are to love God and to love our neighbor (see Matthew 22:37–39). He said the second commandment is *like* the first. We cannot love

God unless we also love our neighbor. The apostle John pulled no punches when he wrote, "If anyone says, 'I love God,' and hates his brother, he is a liar; for he who does not love his brother whom he has seen, cannot love God whom he has not seen" (1 John 4:20).

You and I are in a conundrum. In order to be at peace, we need to love other people. At the same time, it is other people who rob us of our peace! We want to believe that if we do the right thing, and if we can get the other person to do the right thing, everybody will be at peace. Sometimes it works. Sometimes we can get our child to act responsibly, our spouse to give us the love we want, and our boss to recognize our achievements. Therefore, sometimes we are at peace—when things are going our way. This is the human way of finding peace by getting the results we want first.

Jesus' way is the opposite: peace first, results second. By first getting neutral—*before* we quit our job, leave our marriage, or send an angry e-mail—we are practicing peace first, results second. Does this approach feel fatalistic? Does it feel laissez-faire? It is, in a certain way. We are accepting that what happens next is not in our hands. We do our part and then God makes things right according to his will. We pray this in the Lord's Prayer: "Thy will be done on earth as it is in heaven." When we do peace first, results second, we are acting as if we believe that holy prayer.

This is not as laissez-faire as you might think. You still have to act. You still have to do something to deal with the stack of unpaid bills, the unhappy love life, or the boring job. Your choices still have a powerful influence on the results. You knew that. What you perhaps did not know is that Jesus' spiritual teaching provides you with a trustworthy way to clearly see what you need to do. This happens because when you follow Matthew 7:5, you experience the sacred presence of the Holy Spirit—the Counselor or Advocate, as Jesus called him. The Holy Spirit prompts you on how to wisely respond to life-size challenges. However, you can discern these prompts only if you are at peace. Otherwise, the noise in your brain and the turmoil in your heart block out the Spirit and you are left to make a human choice on your own strength, not a sacred, God-centered choice.

You don't have to be a Christian to know this spiritual truth works. The fact is you have already used the Peace Promise many times. Consider the earlier example of making a major financial decision, such as buying a car or a house. When you know the price point at which you are prepared to walk away, you have found neutral.

When you know your point of indifference, you will make a good decision whether you buy or not, as long as you are truly neutral. This same principle applies to every important decision in your life. In fact, Abram used the principle of being neutral in the very first book of the

Bible by being at peace about an uncertain outcome and expressing his reasoning plainly:

> Then Abram said to Lot, "Let there be no strife between you and me, and between your herdsmen and my herdsmen, for we are kinsmen. Is not the whole land before you? Separate yourself from me. If you take the left hand, then I will go to the right; or if you take the right hand, then I will go to the left." (Genesis 13:8–9)

The old saying "I need to sleep on it" also reflects our desire to make wise decisions by first being neutral. We make better decisions when we have some objectivity and distance from the issue. This is easy when we are indifferent about decisions such as which restaurant to go to or what movie to watch. It is much more difficult to do when we are responding to a personal attack from a coworker, or when ex-lovers make false accusations to make us look bad and portray themselves as innocent victims.

To gracefully resolve troubling issues, you need to become skilled at naming the cherished outcomes that you fear may be lost. You must become conscious of how your attachment to these outcomes biases your ability to see your situation with spiritually clear eyes.

Take a moment now to pull out a pen and paper. The following seven questions will guide you toward clarifying troubling issues that are stealing your peace.

1. Name a troubling issue that bothers you.
2. What is the outcome you're getting now?
3. What is the outcome you want?
4. Write out key actions you have taken so far.
5. Which ones showed some promise?
6. Which ones had no effect or made things worse?
7. What are you afraid would happen if you accepted the very outcome you don't want?

The goal of this exercise is to clarify the issue troubling you. The final question asks you to look squarely at what you fear the most. This is a vital part of practicing Matthew 7:5. It involves courageous effort and a genuine desire to resolve a troubling issue. Many people give up quickly, unwilling to make the personal changes needed. They would rather be unhappy than have the enduring peace of Christ.

If you want to live from the deepest place in your soul, practicing Matthew 7:5 offers wonderful rewards that keep building with time and experience. Let me share some of these with you.

SIX

The Rewards of His Peace

The most noticeable benefit of inner peace is the positive effect on your physical health. The absence of stress and adrenaline restores your body's well-being. When I was thirty-five years old, my heart rate and blood pressure were normal at 70 beats per minute and 120 over 80. Five years later, my heart rate dropped to 52 bpm and my blood pressure to 90 over 60, a remarkable improvement. Both remained there for fifteen years and only recently has there been a modest rise in these figures. Even more surprising is that throughout many of those years, I stopped formal exercise, merely remaining active and eating healthily. Of course, the older you are when you begin to bathe your body in inner peace, the more entrenched your health situation may be. Indeed, a debilitating health problem is often God's most powerful way of drawing us near to him.

Deep inner peace also has a dramatic effect on your mental health. We are happier and cope with crises large and small more easily. Of course, we need to navigate a few crises to gain this depth of peace. I am always amazed by people who have faced the greatest crises, such as becoming a paraplegic, and come out of them with a remarkably positive attitude. Life has forced them to become unattached to the hopes and dreams most of us have. They have learned to be grateful for what they do have.

Peace means your mind is no longer preoccupied. You become able to listen to others easily and for long periods of time. When I was a stressed-out corporate executive, I was a poor listener and found it exhausting to do it well. When people's eyes glaze over, you know they have tuned out. Listening well is actually dangerous because you might hear something you don't want to hear, something that disturbs the way you want to believe the world works. With peace first, you can listen to another person's emotional divorce story or inflammatory opinions without needing to argue or tell your story.

A poor listener has a poor recall of conversations and events. You cannot remember something for which you were mentally absent! By age forty, many people complain they no longer remember things as well as before; in reality, they are simply not present. Their mind is swamped with to-do lists, love-life troubles, or worries about career, money, and what others think of them. Overthinking closes your ears the way eyelids close your eyes. A peaceful, present mind retains information with surprisingly little effort. Even trying too hard to remember a name or phone number can cause the information to sit agonizingly on the tip of your tongue. When you become neutral about not remembering, the information will often pop back into your mind effortlessly. This is a simple, common example of Matthew 7:5 working. I find these to be small miracles. "Thank you, Lord," I breathe when they happen.

For people who are analytical by nature, embracing the peace of Christ all day, every day is both appealing and repulsive. We love to think, even as we wish we could shut down the gray beast once in a while! Thinking gives us the ego-based delusion that we are in control as we analyze problems, weigh possible solutions, and imagine how good we will feel if and when we are successful. One driven businesswoman in search of inner peace said to me, "I could readily live in my head all day, every day!"

As you become more neutral, you will create mental space in which to have thoughts about what is actually happening in front of you. You become aware and appreciative of your surroundings. You will notice the roses and smell them, too. You will become much more curious without assuming or jumping to unwise conclusions. You won't need to overanalyze your problems. You will trust that the answer will appear to you just in time. You will perform sexually with ease, comfortable with your body and undistracted by self-conscious anxiety. Sexuality is an enormous cause of peace-robbing beliefs about self-worth. This reward alone makes the pursuit of his peace so worthwhile.

Emotionally, you become centered and grounded most of the time. Attacks from others no longer shame or embarrass you. Life's surprises won't upset you for long. You will see the humor in most situations. You will empathize with the pain of others, and this, combined with your open mind, will allow you to "read" others much better. By the words and tone people use, they reveal much about their inner life and their belief system. You will gain an immediate glimpse into their true motives. I have learned over the years to tread carefully with this ability. If you ask a question or make a comment that is too close to a person's hidden truth, he or she may feel unsafe and flee. You need to discern how frank to be, with an eye toward being helpful with where this person is at, unbiased by a desire to rescue or to show how clever you are.

Spiritually, you become conscious of the prompts of the Holy Spirit. Every person has experienced a "gut" feeling—an intuitive sense of what you need to do here and now.

This is not your logical mind arriving at a conclusion. This is not your heart expressing an emotion of joy or fear or sadness. This is your soul nudging you toward the spiritual answer that is right for you. No one else can tell you this answer. It is between God and you alone.

My most frequent regrets are the ones in which I had a clear "inner knowing" and decided to ignore it. On one occasion, my former wife had a parking lot fender bender. The bolt on her license plate touched the other driver's bumper, leaving a small circular imprint. After a few moments, I had a sense that I should take photos of the scene. I didn't. My logical, biased mind was concerned that the other person, a fellow church member, would take it as a sign of distrust. Later, he wanted to claim damages that were unrelated to her small indentation. The lack of photos made it difficult to readily resolve the matter.

Trusting your inner knowing is a key sign of your spiritual maturity. A still mind is receptive to discerning the voice of God, as inaudible as it usually is. Knowing what you need to do and then doing it is the step of faith that Matthew 7:5 demands of you. As you do it, you experience God's hand in the results you get. You learn that you can trust the future to him if you do your part today.

As you stop dwelling on problems, worrying about money matters, or thinking unkind thoughts about people who hurt you, you notice your mind focuses more on loving God and others. In the book of Revelation, the apostle John describes what this looks like in heaven: "And I heard every creature in heaven and on earth, and under the earth and in the sea, and all therein, saying, 'To him who sits upon the throne and to the Lamb be blessing and honor and glory and might for ever and ever!'" (Revelation 5:13).

A song dances in your heart. You feel joy and thanksgiving that God truly loves you, an imperfect person, just as you are now. Obstacles and trials are his opportunities for you to trust him more fully. The person who hurt you may well turn out to be someone who needs your help. Or he or she may be God's way of helping you learn to stand your ground or give something away that you cherish. When you are unattached to outcomes, you accept that you don't know how things will unfold. You know only that somehow, good will come from the bad if you do your part wisely. These are the steps in life that God has given to you, to be walked unbiased by vengeance, victimization, or victory based on your own definition of what's right.

In *The Non-Judgmental Christian*, I describe our transformation as we live with a focus on God's will for us in troubling situations. We begin our spiritual journey looking like a watermelon. We take up a lot of space, as revealed by the many things that upset us that are actually not ours to fix or change. We have a tough outer shell, as evidenced by our rigid views, especially toward those who don't do things right. Underneath our shell, we are pink mush. We feel hurt and sensitive when someone penetrates our outer boundaries with a well-placed rejection, attack, or abandonment. This is the core reason we find it hard to forgive hurts from others. We fear opening ourselves to a repeated thrust of the knife.

As we practice first being neutral before taking action, we metamorphose into a peach. We take up very little space. We stop taking things personally or worrying about things that are not ours to control. We are soft on the outside, showing compassion to those feeling pain without a desire to fix their pain so that we don't have to feel it or live with it. In our core being, we are tough, like the pit of a peach. We confidently stand our ground on important matters, and the integrity of our soul is not for sale, even in small matters such as lying about our purchases at a border crossing. We are shrinking our boundaries, which leaves us with less to defend and therefore less to fear. Forgiveness becomes easy as our ego becomes unattached to outcomes and to how other people choose to behave.

You are acquiring the mind of Jesus—the Jesus attitude. You are living as if you have nothing to hide, nothing to prove, and nothing to lose. The key word is *nothing*. Paul described this brilliantly in Philippians 2:5–9 (NIV):

> Your attitude should be the same as that of Christ Jesus: Who, being in very nature God, did not consider equality with God something to be grasped, but made himself *nothing*, taking the very nature of a servant, being made in human likeness. And being found in appearance as a man, he humbled himself and became obedient to death—even death on a cross! Therefore God exalted him to the highest place and gave him the name that is above every name.

The Peace Promise leads us toward embracing our nothingness so that we can see what we need to do with the clear eyes of Jesus. As we do, we become neutral about wrongdoings even while they are happening. We have *pre-forgiven* people with specks, just as we are already forgiven by the grace of God—a grace we cannot earn but can only humbly accept. Without a plank in our eye, we see the pain motivating others to do hurtful things. We feel compassion for them without letting pity move us to respond unwisely to those who would trespass against us. Pre-forgiven is the highest level of forgiveness possible. Jesus showed this while dying on the cross when he said, "Father, forgive them; for they know not what they do" (Luke 23:34).

Leaning on Matthew 7:5 takes us on an inch-by-inch spiritual journey through our mind, our heart, and our soul. We move from self-absorbed to selfless—the place where joy finally sustains itself from within. We free our mind from peace-robbing beliefs when we choose to have nothing to hide. We free our heart from the heavy burden of condemnation when we have nothing to prove. We heal our soul of arctic emptiness when we humbly give away personal power as if we have nothing to lose.

When we are at peace that our life is unfolding according to God's will and that we are fulfilling the reason we were born, I believe these words from Jesus come true: "Nor will people say, 'Here it is,' or 'There it is,' because the kingdom of God is in your midst." (Luke 17:21, NIV).

The purpose of our spiritual journey is to find the kingdom of God within us. He is the source of love. We are loved. We cannot love ourselves into happiness. We can only love God and open ourselves to allow his eternal, bottomless love to enter us. "You will keep in perfect peace those whose minds are steadfast, because they trust in you" (Isaiah 26:3, NIV).

Now let us explore the number one obstacle that blinds you from spiritually seeing clearly how to respond to troubling issues that are burdening your heart and stealing your peace.

PART THREE

Let His Peace In

SEVEN

Hundreds of Hidden Beliefs

Unhappiness is how we know that things are not right, and it motivates us to take action to make those things that trouble us right. The only problem is that we can take unwise action that fails. When we try and fail repeatedly, our confidence gets rattled. We can become stuck in a rut, "like a grave with the ends knocked out."

To see a difficult situation with spiritually clear eyes, you need to dig out your biases that make up the plank in your eye. You do this by first becoming conscious of what's going on in your mind. When you do, you will discover a mountain of beliefs—the first barrier to reaping his holy peace.

In the beginning of my spiritual journey, becoming aware of my beliefs was a stunning and life-changing revelation. Little did I know that I held *hundreds* of beliefs hidden in my unconscious mind. Most of them were characterized by the word *should*. Men should do house repairs. Women should do the cooking. Girls shouldn't play football. Public servants should be paid less than private workers. A new car should start every time. Companies should guarantee free replacement of defective products. People should be paid the same wages for the same work. People should be nice to one another (whatever that actually means). Most of these had nothing to do with the Bible and everything to do with customs, conventions, and norms. Beliefs are "the way we do things around here." They are what define us and the culture in which we live.

Of course, we also hold many beliefs that are based on religious teachings. Couples are not to have premarital sex. Abortion is murder. Stealing is bad. Gossiping is a sin. Adultery is wrong. The entire Bible can be viewed as God's rule book. Becoming conscious of all our beliefs, regardless of their source, is the key to discovering which biased plank is blinding us from seeing clearly what to do. Jesus attacked many religious beliefs, such as not picking grain on the Sabbath, saying, "I desire mercy, not sacrifice," to make clear what's important: loving people, not blindly following rules (see Matthew 12:7).

Removing a plank means getting neutral about what you believe in. It doesn't mean you stop *having* beliefs. It means you detach yourself from them. It means hugging and loving someone returning from having an abortion even as you deplore the sin she just committed. You hold the belief yet you are neutral about whether others hold the same belief. Until you get to this hallowed state of mind, your beliefs and your existential being are one and the same. Separating them is how you will be able to not take offenses against your beliefs personally. You will know you get what this means when you can say, "Father, forgive them, for they know not what they do," even while they are doing it.

Martin Luther King Jr. understood this very well when he delivered this powerful message on loving your enemies at Dexter Avenue Baptist Church on November 17, 1957, in Montgomery, Alabama:

Now there is a final reason I think that Jesus says, "Love your enemies." It is this: that love has within it a redemptive power. And there is a power there that eventually transforms individuals. That's why Jesus says, "Love your enemies." Because if you hate your enemies, you have no way to redeem and to transform your enemies. But if you love your enemies, you will discover that at the very root of love is the power of redemption. You just keep loving people and keep loving them, even though they're mistreating you. Here's the person who is a neighbor, and this person is doing something wrong to you and all of that. Just keep being friendly to that person. Keep loving them. Don't do anything to embarrass them. Just keep loving them, and they can't stand it too long. Oh, they react in many ways in the beginning. They react with bitterness because they're mad because you love them like that. They react with guilt feelings, and sometimes they'll hate you a little more at that transition period, but just keep loving them. And by the power of your love they will break down under the load. That's love, you see. It is redemptive, and this is why Jesus says love. There's something about love that builds up and is creative. There is something about hate that tears down and is destructive. So love your enemies.

Your peace has power. And it is your unconscious beliefs that prevent you from unleashing this spiritual power on those who have hurt you. I once believed I was a bad person if I made someone mad at me. When I became conscious of that belief, I was able to choose to no longer believe it. It was a mental lie I had unconsciously acquired, perhaps as young as three years of age. That belief caused me to worriedly lie awake at night, imagining ways to make things right again. I had no peace because I was attached to an outcome: I wanted people to like me. If they didn't like me, I soon found myself feeling angry or resentful toward them. I was unable to love them unless they loved me, too. When a person of importance didn't like me, I felt stressed, tense, and worried. Telling myself not to worry about it had no effect whatsoever. My peace vaporized at the thought of them, and I felt anxiety in their presence.

As you begin to "see" your beliefs, you become aware that you are virtually incapable of seeing an upsetting event in an unbiased way. Your beliefs distort your mind's eye the way sunglasses filter your view of the landscape. You see what you believe, not the full picture of what is actually happening. Until we become conscious of them, beliefs whip us around like a tail wagging the dog. They cause us to consciously look for evidence that affirms what we believe in, and to reject data that contradicts, blocking out what we don't want to see. We rationalize, justify, and deny—defensive behaviors that scream at us, "Plank in my eye!"

Becoming conscious of our beliefs enables us to wisely discern which ones build up our peace and which ones tear it down. As we do, we learn that we can change our beliefs. This sets us free in often stunning ways. Changing a peace-robbing belief is like shedding a fifty-pound weight from our backs. The relief is immediate and life-giving.

The wonderful side effect is that we also set others free to hold different beliefs without feeling threatened or anxious, even if their beliefs are offensive to us. Jesus expressed this truth by saying, "If anyone hears my sayings and does not keep them, I do not judge him; for I did not come to judge the world but to save the world" (John 12:47).

He loves us even when we don't believe or do what he teaches. He set us free and we need to do the same for ourselves and others, as Martin Luther King Jr. understood so well.

A client experienced the freedom and wisdom that comes from first getting neutral about an unhelpful old belief in a situation that robbed her peace every day. Her seventeen-year-old stepson attended high school in a neighboring town. She happened to work near his bus stop, so she drove him in on the days he was with them. They needed to leave by 7:22 a.m. or risk missing the 7:50 bus. For three years, she got in her car at 7:22 and waited in frustration for him to get in. He would often climb into the car as late as 7:27, whereupon they would barely make the bus. With sixteen traffic lights on the route, the travel time was unpredictable, and the trip was stressful for her.

I helped her get neutral by asserting that getting him to school was not her problem but rather *his* problem. This change in belief altered everything for her. She suddenly saw with new eyes what to do. She let him know she would be ready to go whenever he indicated he was ready. She began to relax in the house while he rushed to get ready. If he missed the bus, he knew he would have to take the city bus to school. This was a natural consequence— the best kind to motivate change in others.

She had a common parental bias—that she was responsible for getting him to the bus stop on time. Furthermore, she had the added anxiety of disliking confrontation. When she became neutral about the outcome of whether he arrived on time, she changed her whole approach. He, in turn, was affected and began to get ready on time without anyone being frustrated or unhappy. Inner peace was her reward, while her stepson learned to be responsible for his own timeliness.

This small example illustrates how blurriness about what we are responsible for is a root cause of much anxiety. Beliefs are the rule book by which we decide whether something is ours to fix. For this reason, scrutinizing your belief system is vital to letting the peace of Christ enter your being. Each negative belief is like a brick, blocking out God's life-giving love.

Beliefs are what make us happy or unhappy, not life events or the other person's behavior. Many of us do not realize that the reason we are unhappy is because what's happening is disturbing our belief system. The example of the man who was late for work in chapter three is a good example of how this works. We interpret a troublesome situation through our belief system in order to decide if we are worthy of being loved, respected, and protected from pain. Our ego thinks that if we were worthy, people would respect what we believe and even do what we believe is right. When they don't, we take it personally, aghast at their inability to see the world the right way— our way. This is every bit as true about religious beliefs as it is about any other. That is why it is so powerful to read about how Jesus did not judge those who rejected his beliefs and teachings. Instead, he kept loving them.

Since there is no peace without love, you must sever the link between your beliefs and your existential self-worth. God loves you even if others clash with your beliefs about the right way to do things. Furthermore, this severance is the key to seeing their beliefs—which opens your eyes to possibly removing the speck from their eye. You will never see how to influence others so long as your heart resents the way they see the world. Their beliefs serve them just as yours serve you. Once you get this, you will have compassion rather than judgment for them.

Beliefs are hidden from your awareness. All you see is a right way to clean the house, drive a car, spend money, run a business, and be loved by family members. Beliefs are your life lessons for how to get the results you want. Your parents trained you to believe that if you wanted to be loved by them, you needed to do well in school and keep your room tidy. Your spouse trained you to believe that you need to be sensitive to his or her needs. In the same way, you have trained your spouse in how you want to be treated. We each extend and withdraw our love, carrot-and-stick style, to get what we want from others. In this way, love and fear become weapons to enforce our belief system.

When people trespass against our belief system, we let them know in a variety of ways, often through tone of voice and facial expressions. "Honey, where did you put my shoes?" You can say this lovingly or snarl it at your wife. If you snarl, she will get the message loud and clear: Your shoes are lost and it's her fault. In this case, you have a belief about where your shoes ought to be left and whose fault it is.

Another common trespass is lateness and waiting. We want results in *our* timing, not when others get around to it! Even if we try to disguise our annoyance or anger, most people will pick up on our tone, especially those who know us intimately well.

Do others respond to our disapproval with thanks and gratitude? Rarely. Instead, they deny the truth of their actions, become defensive, or deflect the subject to another topic. I call these the three Ds: deny, defend, deflect. If we are observant, we will notice that others dig in even more, stubbornly refusing to change because they know we are pressuring them to do so, like the wayward husband in chapter one. This is the human ego in play, a reaction I call the "opposite effect." Our biased view makes things worse, not better. It is like pouring gasoline onto a fire we desperately want to put out. Jesus warned us this would be true when he said, "the measure you give will be the measure you get" (Matthew 7:2). Judgments cause people to want to judge us right back, rather than remove the speck we are pointing out to them.

Making matters worse, we often become even more determined to enforce our biases to get the outcome we want. We decide to add some bite to our bark. We think that if we inflict a painful enough consequence, people will change. If someone cuts us off while we're driving, a dirty look will show them the error of their ways. And if that doesn't work, then speeding ahead and cutting them off in return will surely be successful. "That'll teach 'em!" we say, pumping our fist with satisfaction. We want them to know how it feels to be hurt the way we feel hurt.

Sometimes this approach does work. Sometimes, if we bark loudly enough, our spouse, parent, or child will stop his or her frustrating behavior. Indeed, the law and police work is based on the principle that punitive consequences will keep people in line. For weak leaders in particular, might makes right. People may appear to cooperate but only with their actions, not their hearts. Instead, they silently resent being pressured and let others know how they feel in a passive-aggressive way.

When people pressure us to change, our ego becomes inflamed. Just try pushing a slow driver to speed up by sitting on his bumper, and watch what happens. Does he speed up? Rarely! Instead, he slows down even more. Over the course of history, many revolutions have been rooted in resistance to being kept in line. We are aware that others may angrily retaliate if we take a strong stand on what we believe. This sends our stress and anxiety soaring, causing us to shrink back or defiantly bulldoze onward. This is the link to boundaries.

As we practice the Peace Promise, we realize that no one is "making" us do anything. We are always choosing, based on what we believe and the consequences we are willing to accept. We discover we can retain peace-building beliefs and let go of peace-robbing ones.

I have experienced great relief countless times by changing peace-robbing beliefs, including:

- I'm a loser if I make a mistake.
- Fat people, especially overweight women, are repulsive.
- God wants me to be poor and single.
- People with more money are better than I am.
- When someone asks me a question, I am supposed to have the right answer.
- When someone criticizes me, I'm stupid.
- Other people can make me unhappy.
- I would rather not try than try and fail.

These beliefs are mere samples from the massive, unconscious rule book I built about how to live a successful life, be accepted by groups I wanted to belong to, and please those who mattered to me.

Beliefs cause us to judge people. We unconsciously compare what people say and do to our belief about right and wrong in that situation. Then we condemn the wrongdoer, be it the other person or ourself, whether silently or out loud.

Judgments hurt. To protect ourselves from the pain, we look for ways to rationalize what we've done by putting the blame on others. Or we selectively recall only the good things we've done. I spent countless hours replaying past events, looking for ways to justify myself. I role-played imaginary future conversations with people whose approval I craved, looking for ways to come out of messy situations looking like the good guy. Similarly, I fantasized about how impressed they would be if I said witty things or did amazing feats.

The mental gymnastics of replaying, role-playing, and fantasizing stole my peace for decades. I was endlessly feeding an insatiable ego-based desire to be good enough in the eyes of others to earn their love and affection. I also used these gyrations to justify dumping people whom I deemed unworthy of my friendship and support.

Beliefs fill our minds with expectations about how others ought to behave. I recall having conversations in my head with my first wife about wanting to go golfing, deciding she would not agree, and then getting mad at her, all while never having voiced my desire in the first place! How unfair that was to her. However, I was too self-absorbed to even notice that this was my pattern. My expectations of how others should respond to me weakened my performance and rattled my confidence when things did not go as planned. Lost in my overthinking, analytical mind was John Kuypers, control freak, trying to anticipate every problem, cover every angle, and manage what others thought of me.

Beliefs prevent us from being fully present when our encounters with others actually take place. When we are caught by surprise by others, we are unable to respond right in the moment from a place of love. Instead, we feel triggered. We cannot be serious about reaping his peace until we become aware of how much we want to stamp out the specks in people who endanger the outcomes we crave, such as approval, respect, money, and love.

When we identify and change our peace-robbing beliefs, we give ourselves the remarkable ability to change our inner experience without changing the circumstances themselves. By becoming neutral about the outcome we want, we let go of judging people as good or bad. Instead, we see people as they are—making mistakes like we do. We accept they have that right, as do we. Furthermore, we become vastly more aware that perhaps we are the ones who have it wrong. This lets us respond in the moment in a nonjudgmental way without feeling like we are endorsing them or needing to protect ourselves. We are not merely eliminating peace-robbing beliefs. Rather, we are replacing them with new, peace-building beliefs.

Jesus said that when you remove the judgment you have about a person whose fault offends you, you will see clearly how to help that person remove his or her fault. You will no longer be spiritually blind. This should be the greatest news you have heard in your entire life! Imagine that you, a person who is not the president of the United States or Superman, could actually remove a fault from someone else.

If you don't feel excited about becoming this spiritually powerful, I think I know why.

You *like* making judgments. You like being able to say, "Hah! I caught you! You said you would [clean the house; have sex with me; promote me to a better job; love me till death do us part] and you didn't do it! You offended me with your insensitive and hurtful actions. My unhappiness is your fault. You are a bad person, and I have every right to be angry with you and unhappy about my life." Judgments help us play the victim, justify holding grudges, and more than anything else, avoid taking responsibility for our own choices and actions.

Let's not deceive ourselves. We love the planks in our eye. We cling to them like a child to a security blanket.

Every time we feel hurt, we tuck a plank into the bottomless terabytes of our memory bank. She lied once. Now she is a liar about everything. He looked at another person with lust. Now he is an adulterer ready to jump into bed with anyone who comes along.

A vicious cycle begins. We use others' faults and mistakes like evidence, pressuring them to do things our way. We want them to know how their speck hurt us and that they need to change their behavior for us to feel better. If they don't, we strike back with a sharp word or we abandon them, unwilling to associate with people who are "like that"—a selfish friend, a mean boss, a rude business owner. We don't see that that their behavior frequently has nothing to do with us. We are merely collateral damage in their hapless search for happiness, selfish as they might be.

Most important, we don't see they are offering us a powerful spiritual path to removing our own planks. St. Paul wrote: "You, therefore, have no excuse, you who pass judgment on someone else, for at whatever point you judge the other, you are condemning yourself, because you who pass judgment do the same things" (Romans 2:1, NIV).

You are guilty of that which offends you in others. It took me two full years to see and believe this spiritual truth. I call it "All I See Is Me." When I judge others, I judge me. When I am offended by others, I am implicitly agreeing that they might be right. Otherwise, what is there for me to be offended about? When I became neutral about their faults, I freed both them and myself from this cycle of misery. They are only doing what I myself have done or would do if I were authentic. Failing to believe this latter point is a massive obstacle to peace. Many clients have self-righteously exclaimed to me, "I would never do what that person did!" If this is true—and it often is—it is only because we use judgments to hold ourselves at bay. This is the greatest fear you will face in letting go of peace-robbing beliefs—the fear that you will do the very thing you judged so harshly in the past.

Until you become neutral about beliefs, your only path to peace is to live in a false bubble where you only associate with people who think like you and agree with you. Church groups are especially prone to this. This is our comfort zone, and it blocks us from loving our more prickly neighbor and hence receiving God's love. Our comfort zone becomes a prison constructed of our beliefs. We try to make our life fit our belief system by condemning or avoiding anyone who doesn't fit in. Those who are depressed often shut everyone out of their lives. Isolation ensures no one rattles their negative belief system.

The first stage in your pursuit of lasting peace is to examine your mind and the beliefs you hold. It is about self-awareness—that you are always choosing and no one is making you do anything. You will discover that it is your fear of the consequences of not conforming to expectations that robs you of your peace. When you drop peace-robbing beliefs that no longer serve you, you experience peace about a troubling issue even if the circumstance itself remains the same. In so doing, you set yourself free to see new ways to remove the speck from the eye of those you love, if you even see a speck once you get past your own plank.

In chapter eight, we will look at the three stages of the spiritual journey we all need to travel if we want to reap the full bounty of his peace.

EIGHT

The Three Nothings

In the experience with my father in chapter three, blaming him was my way of not taking responsibility for my role in our estranged relationship. I saw his specks and I was blind to the plank in my eye. Once you become real, you become acutely aware of the choices you are making, and you take ownership of them. You can no longer deny that you chose not to turn the other cheek and instead lashed out at someone. You are making a major shift from being self-absorbed to being self-aware—of your habits and choices caused by the beliefs in your mind. Your beliefs are revealed to you when you choose to live with nothing to hide. The first nothing is stage one of the journey to harvest Jesus' peace. It is the first of the three layers that comprise the plank in our eye.

The second stage is when we have something to prove. This layer comprises the judgments in our heart—the ones that harden us and render us incapable of compassion toward those who hurt us. Judgments are rooted in our desire to prove that we are right—that the other person did it to us and he or she deserves condemnation and punishment. Other people's specks trigger powerful emotions in our heart. Jesus said, "But what comes out of the mouth proceeds from the heart, and this defiles a man" (Matthew 15:18). The judgments in your heart defile you. The evidence is the words that come out of your mouth. You will never have peace until you overcome these judgments. You will experience immeasurable joy when you embrace living as if you have nothing to prove.

Most of us hide our judgments behind a carefully constructed mask. It hides our heart's true desire—to take control of getting what we want and let those who stand in our way know what we really think of them. The Jim Carrey movie *Liar Liar* does a lovely job of parodying this truth. Our authentic self has lustful thoughts. We have real feelings of envy when others get things we cannot afford; we feel we'll never have their good fortune. We get fed up with being rejected by prospective lovers, employers, and social groups. Our real self gets angry, sad, and scared. The job of Protector is to keep our truth carefully hidden because we know that people will react badly if we openly reveal the dark side of our personality.

Jesus had no such fear. He lived and taught as if he had nothing to prove, even as he sought to teach people God's truth. His adversaries recognized this: "'Teacher,' they said, 'we know that you are a man of integrity and that you teach the way of God in accordance with the truth. You aren't swayed by others because you pay no attention to who they are'" (Matthew 22:16, NIV).

They saw that Jesus was not worried in the least about what people thought of him and therefore could be entirely trusted. He had nothing to prove. He spoke his truth. People could believe him or not—that was up to them. He was neutral about pressuring them but he was in no way without strong feelings. To me, the saddest passage in the entire Bible is when Jesus was sentenced to death and about to carry his cross. He said, "For if they do this when the wood is green, what will happen when it is dry?" (Luke 23:31). He mourned the people he had come to save and their horrible ignorance. God himself was in their very presence and they were sentencing him to die. I weep at the thought.

People who have nothing to prove do not distort or manipulate the truth. Neither do they shame or criticize others into agreeing with them. They speak their truth boldly and are not easily upset. They have this ability because their hearts are neutral about the outcomes at stake. Their words and tone are not laced with personal attacks and innuendos. They do not compare, criticize, or condemn differences compared to their own beliefs and expectations.

By contrast, people with something to prove eagerly seek the approval of others, selling their point of view hard and feeling upset if others disagree or fail to be impressed. This upset reveals itself in the form of judgment. We see this commonly in social media, where people can hide their identities while lobbing personal attacks at others. Rather than loving others, they are pressuring others to agree with them. They may resentfully comply or put up a wall to shut people out. I had such a wall with my father. Each and every judgment is like a brick in the wall that separates us from the peace of our real Father in heaven.

An emotional and spiritual transformation happens when we vulnerably remove the judgmental wall around our heart. We become compassionate. We stop reacting every time someone zings us or does something we dislike. We see with new eyes why they do what they are doing, even if we profoundly disagree with them. We learn to care less about being right and love more who that person is, flaws and all. This second nothing pushes us toward self-acceptance. When we accept our faults, we gain compassion for the faults of others. Instead of seeing people as mean or bad, we see lost, broken individuals desperately looking for love and acceptance, just as we have done so often. We become capable of authentic empathy. We are them. They are us.

Jesus was asked why Moses permitted divorce. He replied, "For your hardness of heart [Moses] wrote you this commandment" (Mark 10:5). This hardening of the heart is rooted in biased views about someone we once loved. We think this person doesn't love us and perhaps never did. Otherwise, why would he or she treat us so? Having nothing to prove helps us accept that we are imperfect and so are those we love. We become capable of listening without feeling impulsively compelled to deny, defend, or deflect (the three Ds) in the face of their accusations. Our hearts soften and we resolve differences calmly. The price of this stage of our journey is to acknowledge we had more of a role to play in the creation of the troubling issue than we previously cared or dared to admit. We experience humility and a broken spirit. A softer heart is our reward.

As you continue to practice Matthew 7:5, perhaps after several years you will find yourself torn yet again. God will push you into the third stage of the spiritual journey that leads to his peace: to live as if you have nothing to lose. While you now accept your faults and those of others, you will remain at odds with some people who matter to you.

You will hit granite-like hard spots in which changing your beliefs about what is right and wrong is no longer an option. You will have done the work and know what you believe is right for you. You now become unwilling to give these away. You solidify your beliefs about lifestyle, finances, parenting, and marriage. Unless your spouse, children, or employer shift some of their deeply held views, you will face major unresolved differences, as I did in my second marriage. These are no longer polluted by negative conflicts but are peppered instead with honest dialogue and unhappy stalemates. Something has to give. At this point, you have something to lose.

All great movies and novels depend on the main characters having something precious to lose—a child, a fortune, or a great achievement, for example. The things we value, such as money, reputation, marriage, and our position in the work world, bias our responses when we feel threatened by their loss. They are part of our core identity. We blend our identity with our job title, neighborhood, wealth, citizenship, race, faith affiliation, and marital status. Losing these feels like losing a part of who we are.

For people with addictions, their habit is deeply connected to their sense of identity, such as "I am a smoker." When I struggled to quit smoking cigarettes, I became conscious that I was a smoker only while I was smoking. When I butted out, I was no longer a smoker. Each time I lit a cigarette, I reminded myself, "I am choosing to smoke." This is linked to being present, or conscious that we are always choosing and that habits do not control us—we control them, but not on our own strength. The apostle Paul described how he learned to endure good times and bad:

> I know what it is to be in need, and I know what it is to have plenty. I have learned the secret of being content in any and every situation, whether well fed or hungry, whether living in plenty or in want. I can do all this through him who gives me strength. (Philippians 4:12–13, NIV)

Having something to lose is the third and deepest level of the plank in our eye. We face power struggles that are ultimately centered on just one question: Who gets to decide? Couples face this regularly. One wants children; the other does not. One wants out of the rat race; the other wants a fast-paced career. One wants to winter in Florida; the other wants to stay close to home. One wants financial security in the future; the other wants to spend money to enjoy the good things in life *now*. Each has a dream that is central to his or her being. We are fighting for our very lives, our sense of identity. Some married people experience this as if they are dying inside. One partner's victory is the other partner's loss. Win-win seems nigh impossible. This stage centers on a great power struggle, one we now intentionally choose to lose.

We are being forced to let go of our attachments to our dreams. Someone has to give. Circumstances might force it, such as with a life-threatening illness, or we can intentionally choose to give away power. When our marriage is in trouble, we are forced to consider what matters more: adapting to our present partner or pursuing a "better" lover. When we lose our job, we are forced to change our lifestyle or spend our savings. When our reputation is attacked, we are forced to let go of what others think of us or lie awake in torment about something we cannot control. When our health is in danger, our need to change skyrockets and so does our anxiety. To become neutral about losing our dreams is existentially disturbing. However, the sooner you are prepared to put these precious attachments on the table, the sooner you will clearly see what you need to do.

As we face each loss, it looks like proof that God does not love us and neither do our spouses, parents, or children. We feel like a suffering loser. Our desire to fight hard to keep what we don't want to lose leads to many great struggles and much unhappiness. We face our deepest fear that we are inherently unlovable. As we travel this dark stage, we experience an unexpected reward: permanent inner healing. God surgically removes our inner pain in this stage by making us face our deepest fear that we will never be loved the way we deserve. Our lover will never be who we wish. Our parents will always be who they are.

Our career will be permanently damaged. Our friend has left us forever.

What we cannot know or truly believe until after we do it is that losing is the key to winning. Only when we give until it hurts do we gain the love that we were seeking. St. Teresa of Calcutta is quoted as having said, "I have found the paradox that if you love until it hurts, there can be no more hurt, only more love." Jesus expressed it this way: "Whoever seeks to gain his life will lose it, but whoever loses their life will preserve it" (Luke 17:33). We must die to self. When we do, we discover that we have healed our deepest inborn wound. We accept that part of us that is unacceptable, the part that never felt good enough when we were a child. We resolve life's greatest dilemma exactly as Paul Tillich described in *The Courage to Be*. Nowhere is this healing process more valid and alive than in our marriage. Choosing to lose is the spiritual key to creating the love relationship of your dreams. In my case, it meant accepting the end of my marriage. I believe leaving is what my former wife, an unbeliever, needed in order for the Lord to work in her life. I accept this as best for her and for me, even though I don't believe God wants marriages to end. Her eternal salvation is more important than our temporal marriage. St. Paul wrote:

But if the unbelieving partner desires to separate, let it be so; in such a case the brother or the sister is not bound. For God has called us to peace. Wife, how do you know whether you

will save your husband? Husband, how do you know whether
you will save your wife? (1 Corinthians 7:15–16)

During this third stage of our spiritual journey, we
receive peace in our soul. We move from self-acceptance to
inner healing. With nothing to lose, you are truly trusting
that God will make all things right in his timing. You cannot
know this in your bones until you actually give away real
decision-making power. This is how you will experience
the humility that is foundational to experiencing his peace.

The Holy Spirit gave me the strength to intentionally
endure a soul-ravaging stage with my former wife for two
long years, in the eighth and ninth years of our sixteen-
year marriage. When it was over—when I had given away
as much control as I could—she felt safer and more loved.
One day, she suddenly began giving me the very thing I had
always wanted but rarely received—a genuine interest in
my world. Paradoxically, I no longer needed it. The old me
would have resentfully gasped, "Finally! What *took* you so
long?" Instead, God's wise ways shone through. I realized
that this had been her purpose in my spiritual journey all
along. I once was blind but now I could gratefully see and
accept her changes as God's grace. I needed to learn how to
need nothing from her.

This same experience has repeated itself for me many
times with friends, family members, colleagues, and
neighbors. You need to get neutral about what they are

doing and how they affect you. Only then can you see clearly what to do. You learn to trust with wonderment that God will have his purpose hidden in your troubling issue. Your reward is the gift of an untroubled heart.

To get neutral about outcomes so you can see clearly what to do, you need to have nothing to hide, nothing to prove, and nothing to lose—the Jesus attitude. The following chart maps out the spiritual journey that unfolds when you practice Matthew 7:5 consistently over time.

The Inner Peace Mission: A Spiritual Journey					
	Pre-Stage	Stage 1	Stage 2	Stage 3	Post-Stage
Inner Change	Self-absorbed	Self-aware	Self-accepting	Self-healing	Self-less
Boundary Lines	Something to hide, prove, lose	Nothing to hide	Nothing to prove	Nothing to lose	Three nothings = love
Level of Inner Peace	Body pain and anxiety	Peace of mind	Peace of heart	Peace of soul	Constant inner peace
Action	Unconscious habit-driven	Change hidden beliefs	Own your role	Give away power	Servant leader
Transformation	Human attitude		→→→		Jesus attitude
Learning Books	*The Peace Promise*	*What's Important Now*	*The Non-Judgmental Christian*	*Who's the Driver Anyway?*	

I invite you to take a moment right now and apply the three nothings to a troubling situation in your life. Is there something you need to say that you are hiding? Is there an injustice that you want to prove to someone? What do you have to lose that is precious if things don't work out the way you want?

Finally, ask yourself, "What is the one solution that I truly do not want to consider?" The odds are you don't want to pay a price you feel is unjust. Jesus said, "But I say to you, Love your enemies, and pray for those who persecute you" (Matthew 5:44). To love and pray for the well-being of someone who has hurt you, and even give a kindness to him or her, feels undeserved and unjust. In 2006, the Amish community in Lancaster County, Pennsylvania, demonstrated this when they forgave the man who murdered five of their innocent young daughters in a schoolhouse invasion and then killed himself. More than thirty-five Amish attended his funeral, including parents of the deceased. The world was stunned at this act of love.

When you can live with the worst-case scenario—that you will never get the outcome you truly want—you become free. You become neutral about *all* outcomes on that issue. You develop the wisdom to trust the Holy Spirit, open your eyes to see new ways to act, and possess newfound courage. God's grace will appear in tangible ways and your heart will be gladdened with joy.

Let us examine the two ways in which God will help you successfully apply the Peace Promise so that you can reap his peace.

NINE

Two Ways to Successfully Apply the Peace Promise

The most powerful way to apply Jesus' wise teaching in Matthew 7:5 is in a real-life situation; this reactive approach is intense and pressing. You are in pain and you want relief now. Perhaps you and your spouse are hammering at each other or giving each other the cold shoulder. You want a solution badly, but your willingness to first get neutral will be low. Your emotions are high, and you want the other person to do the right thing: own up, make up, and take responsibility. Your capacity to first get neutral will be at its very weakest, perhaps even nonexistent. You are trapped behind human eyes that cannot see a way out of the vortex of darkness.

In marriage, fights can quickly escalate into hailstorms. A simple issue such as how to decorate a child's bedroom can become a fight that feels deeply personal. "How come we have to do it your way? . . . What do you mean, that's an insult? I simply said I disagree with your suggestion and offered an alternative!" "You didn't just disagree. You yelled at me!"

We lose sight of the issue in seconds, as it becomes buried in a flurry of judgmental accusations. Each volley is indicative of deeper issues we bring in from our past—hurts from previous relationships and wounds from the way our parents raised us. We cannot see what is really bothering us underneath the surface issue. We are blinded by large planks of lumber.

The Peace Promise opens our eyes to this destructive pattern. Increasingly, we become able to quickly put the brakes on a looming hailstorm by naming it as such. Then we can return to the issue at hand, blocking out all the dangling sidebars. Often, it is embarrassingly unimportant, such as where to hang this child's prized trophy versus that child's trophy, or whether you heard each other's words accurately.

For me, one of my deepest triggers lay hidden in these hailstorms—that of not feeling heard. This was an old problem stemming from my childhood with two preoccupied, workaholic farming parents. Matthew 7:5 helped me see with new eyes that it was OK to repeat myself if needed. As I became able to patiently restate my words, my spouse became ever more attentive to making an effort to hear me accurately the first time. A positive cycle began, which we both valued.

In heated emotional situations, you need to bravely look in the mirror and ask yourself some questions: Why does this situation bother you? As with eating an elephant, complex personal relationships need to be resolved one bite at a time or they will be overwhelming in size and scope. My favorite slogan for resolving life-size challenges is "By the yard, it's hard, but by the inch, it's a cinch." I remind myself from thousands of daily lessons that one person's inch is another person's yard. Becoming neutral first gives you the patience to unravel the knots in what is bothering you, digest change, communicate better, and be more considerate of the needs of others.

The second way you can learn the Peace Promise is to proactively uncover biases that trigger you. This approach can be compared to going to a fitness club before you compete in a triathlon; you are preparing to get neutral before unknown future difficulties arise. You intentionally seek to stretch your mental, emotional, and spiritual comfort zones. I also compare this to weeding a garden. Each speck that triggers you is like a weed. If you want constant peace, simply notice and dig out these weeds every day as they come along. I can assure you that the weeding will never stop, but the rewards of a healthy inner garden will also never stop!

I took courses and attended therapy to achieve this goal. During my courses, the instructors intentionally created experiences that reminded us of old wounds that we had buried. The story of my father is one example. It may seem strange to go out of your way to upset yourself, but it is not if you are committed to having more peace in your life today and always. I came to terms with many issues that equipped me to later handle calamities I had no idea awaited me. You are seeking to gain control over your inner experience by purposely exposing those aspects of your mind and heart that cause you to become upset when things do not go your way. In reality, you are digging up your past so that you can stop it from autopiloting your present-moment reactions.

Later in your journey, you will notice more of the everyday moments that trigger you. Consider these: Does traffic frustrate you? Do your kids' habits get under your skin? What about politics and religion? Can you become neutral about taxes you dislike paying? What about people who claim to be spiritual but are often hypocritical? One pastor told me how one of his wealthier church members threatened to leave the church if he didn't agree to put the flowers in the sanctuary in accordance with her wishes.

Remember, you are not learning to be a doormat. You are seeking to be *temporarily* neutral about an issue that bothers you so that you will see clearly what you need to do. Once clear, you are no longer neutral. You are focused and centered. You are ready to speak right in the moment with a young woman about to have an abortion, a friend who is dying of cancer, or a thief who has broken into your house and is threatening your life. The more neutral and at peace you are while the event is actually happening, the more ready you are to let the Holy Spirit direct you in that very moment on what to say or do.

This is the highest reward for those who seek his peace every day for years. Your adult child comes home and announces he is homosexual, and you respond wisely. Your spouse disappoints you, and you quickly get clear about what you need to say and do. Someone at work makes a sharp remark that undermines months of hard work, and you find the right words to put this person in place without stabbing him or her back. You are comfortable in your own skin and at ease around people of any background or personality type. They are pre-forgiven, as I wrote earlier. People see and experience for themselves that something is different about you. Peace is what's different.

A helpful way to apply Matthew 7:5 is to live out the famous Serenity Prayer, written by Christian theologian Reinhold Niebuhr in the 1940s.

O God, grant me the serenity to accept the things I cannot change,

the courage to change the things I can
and the wisdom to know the difference.

By first becoming neutral, we gain the wisdom to know what to accept and what to change. We gain clear, healthy boundaries. We are cured of our spiritual blindness and able to touch others with the power of love. When we are most effective, others do not even notice our role. They think they did it themselves. If we are wise, we will agree with them, not because we are so magnanimous but because it is true! We did what we needed to do and they picked themselves up and did the right thing in response. This is the unshakable evidence that the Holy Spirit is doing the heavy lifting, not you.

Sometimes, getting neutral means you will take a firm stand. When you do, the other person is likely to be unhappy with you for a time. This is like tough love in parenting. Remember, people always want you to agree with their biased view of the "right" answer. Get ready to be tested! When you have neutrality as a foundation, you remain open to the possibility that you have misjudged or made an error. I have failed so often that I am at peace with my shortcomings, even when they're pointed out to me with some passion! This is how we can trust ourselves to do the right thing in the heat of the moment or recover quickly when we fail. We remain centered in God's love for us, making us strong when people unleash their unhappiness on us.

Being neutral about a topic that someone else is passionate about can be surprisingly threatening to that person. Our neutrality disturbs his or her belief system. I believe this is the core spiritual power of neutrality. When we are neutral, we are forcing others to own their choices and their decisions. This is good for them, but some people do not want to take that responsibility. They anxiously need us to agree with their biased views on religion, politics, how to parent a child, and the right way to load the dishwasher.

I have never successfully conveyed the depth and impact of this principle through words and stories alone. People have understood it only when they applied it and learned to trust that Jesus' contrarian teaching actually works. Like all matters that are spiritual, we only truly believe our own experiences. As academic knowledge, the Peace Promise is useless and often rejected by "smart" people. Spirituality is not logical. As British author G. K. Chesterton wrote, "To love means loving the unlovable. To forgive means pardoning the unpardonable. Faith means believing the unbelievable. Hope means hoping when everything seems hopeless."

One great fear of a Christian embracing this teaching is that being neutral will make you a doormat. Was Jesus a doormat? Not even remotely. He spoke fearlessly and acted boldly while his very life was under heavy threat. He knew what to accept and what to change. He was led by the Spirit of God within and was unwavering, even when it meant accepting a humiliating death sentence given only to the worst of criminals.

A particularly striking example of Jesus' fierce inner strength is described in Matthew 15:21–28. A non-Jewish woman cried out to Jesus to heal her daughter. This is the shocking way in which he responded:

> But [Jesus] did not answer her a word. And his disciples came and begged him, saying, "Send her away, for she is crying after us." He answered, "I was sent only to the lost sheep of the house of Israel." But she came and knelt before him, saying, "Lord, help me." And he answered, "It is not fair to take the children's bread and throw it to the dogs." She said, "Yes, Lord, yet even the dogs eat the crumbs that fall from their master's table." Then Jesus answered her, "O woman, great is your faith! Be it done for you as you desire." And her daughter was healed instantly.

Jesus was at peace with her suffering and indifferent to what might happen to her daughter. Even her pleading did not move him. His purpose was to serve the lost sheep of Israel, and on this point, he was unwavering. However, there is a second extraordinary lesson in this Scripture. Only when the woman demonstrated total humility, willing to take any spiritual scrap offered, did Jesus move. Such a vulnerable and total surrender is consistent with my experiences. In order to be neutral about outcomes before the Lord, you need to be 100 percent surrendered if you want God's attention; 99 percent is not enough. It is in our weakness that his strength is revealed to us.

When we let God participate in our decisions, we become open and vulnerable. We lose our desire to fix, repair, or alter people. Instead, we encourage and support them without taking their problems or their rejections personally. We do as Jesus did when two blind men shouted for mercy. This time, he responded, "What do you want me to do for you?" (Matthew 20:32). This was an unbiased, neutral question that neither promised anything nor limited him.

There have been a number of noticeable changes in my daily life as a result of practicing the Peace Promise. One is that I am constantly asking permission of people. "Is this a good time to talk?" "Are you open to a suggestion?" "Would you be willing to help me in one small way?" Another habit I acquired is to default to the assumption that I am wrong and they are right. "I could be wrong about this—I certainly have been many times—but is it possible that there is another way to do this?" "You're probably right about that. I wonder if there is a way to know for sure." I am at peace with my own ignorance and mistakes. When the words that come out of your mouth change, it is proof that your heart has changed.

A third new habit for me is to offer people a way out. "I'd love to go see this movie, but if it doesn't work for you, that's fine with me, too." I give them space and permission to reject me and what I want. I draw them into being authentic by making it safe for them to be truthful. They know I won't be offended. The benefit to me is that I lower the likelihood they will tell me what they think I want to hear, only to change their mind later on or do it out of obligation and not heartfelt desire.

A fourth example is patient persistence. I once had a prospective client cancel our meetings five times over a three-month period. I breezily accepted these last-minute cancellations while offering up a new date that worked for her. When we did finally meet, she was warmly appreciative. These simple habits were once nearly impossible for me to practice in a sincere way. The old me was too attached to getting the results I wanted as fast as I could get them.

When you consistently practice Matthew 7:5, you move through the three spiritual nothings over a period of years. You leave your inherent self-absorbed pre-state and move into self-awareness, then self-acceptance, and finally inner healing. As you seek his peace on your journey, "self" shrinks. Simultaneously, you become more conscious of the greater world around you. You actually begin to feel the pain of others as your compassion grows and your heart softens.

Twentieth-century French Jewish philosopher, teacher, and social activist Simone Weil is said to have cried when she heard about people starving in far-off China. That is empathy and compassion at an extraordinary spiritual level. Martin Luther King Jr. echoed this sentiment when he said, "An individual has not started living until he can rise above the narrow confines of his individualistic concerns to the broader concerns of all humanity." Jesus lived and died for all humanity with no earthly gains for himself along the way.

Let's now look at some extraordinary people of faith who made their own commitment to seeking his peace and what they experienced as a result.

PART FOUR

Stop Resisting

TEN

Experiences of Others

We resist God's peace because accepting it means we have to change. Our resistance becomes our unhappy prison. A friend once complained about how his wife nagged him about his dope-smoking habit. "I just want her to accept me as I am," he moaned.

I responded, "Sure, but you don't accept her any more than she accepts you."

"That's not true," he said indignantly. "If she wants to smoke dope, she can go right ahead!"

"Yes," I said, "you accept that she can smoke but you don't accept that she can nag you!"

He groaned in protest. "That is not the same thing!"

"Yes it is," I persisted. "You want her to accept your fault but you don't want to accept her fault." He rolled his eyes and reluctantly agreed with me. That was the last time I heard that complaint from him.

Accepting another person's fault means accepting the consequence it has on us. It means being vulnerable to emotional pain we don't want and taking responsibility for things we would rather not do. It means accepting that the other person's failure to change is partly our fault because our way of "helping" him hasn't worked. In fact, we are unconsciously making him resist even more, as our biased judgments merely trigger his judgmental desire to further dig in. Ouch. We are blind to our own faults and resist the efforts of others to change us. Like my dope-smoking friend, we just want others to accept us as we are, yet we have no awareness of the cost to them.

When we avoid change or even deny that we need it, we remain blind. God's way of opening our eyes often arrives in the form of hardship. We need our spouse to dump us, our boss to drive us crazy, our friend to betray us, or an addiction to overwhelm us before we do something. Sometimes, we even need the dark cloud of a life-threatening illness.

This happened to a friend in her late fifties who was diagnosed with cancer. Before that, I would have described her as a complainer. She often peppered her conversations with a stream of digs about her husband's habits. She was fed up with her thirty-year-old daughter living at home. She was eager to retire from her long career in public service. Then she got cancer. Amazingly, she started to become a much more positive person. For four years, she battled the cancer. When I saw her three months before she died, she laughed easily and often. She was at peace with her destiny. She said she did not believe in God but was convinced she would end up "somewhere out there in the stars!" Her illness helped her become unattached to life itself, let alone the many small irritants that previously gloomed her days.

Senior executive Eugene O'Kelly had a similar experience in 2005. At age fifty-three, he was the CEO of KPMG in New York City, a global accounting and consulting firm. He started getting severe headaches. Doctors found late-stage brain cancer. He was told he had four months to live. After digesting the devastating news, he decided to write *Chasing Daylight*, a book about his last days on earth.

He became aware that he used to spend his days thinking ahead to the next meeting, the next weekend getaway with his wife, the next stage of his daughter's childhood, and his next success. In other words, he constantly lived in the future. He described his new awareness like this: "Thanks to my situation, I'd attained a new level of awareness, one I didn't possess the first fifty-three years of my life. It's just about impossible for me to imagine going back to that other way of thinking, when this new way enriched me so."[5]

Facing the loss of everything, he discovered the real meaning of life—that it happens now, in the present. Indeed, the present moment is all we have. The future is not ours and never was. A particularly powerful moment occurred when he looked around a cancer treatment waiting room and saw others just like him. At that moment, he forgot about his own situation and felt a deep compassion for their struggles, fears, and losses. He found the true meaning of love. When we are at peace with our own situation, our love for others naturally springs forth.

Compassion and empathy are two of the best gifts we receive when we become neutral, unbiased, and unattached to the outcome of a difficulty we are facing or a fault in someone. O'Kelly accepted his fate and in so doing he found both gifts. The result was a new insight on what he needed to do. He needed to change the way people perceived dying by writing authentically about his death experience.

For centuries, people of faith have experienced freedom, peace, and serenity by becoming neutral and unattached to what might happen before they take action. In the book *Heroic Leadership*, Chris Lowney described how this has happened for 450 years in a "company" called the Society of Jesus, whose members are better known as Jesuits. Lowney explained why this Roman Catholic organization has survived and thrived, outlining four defining characteristics of its leadership: self-awareness, ingenuity, love, and heroism. He pinpointed founder Ignatius of Loyola's spiritual exercises as the main platform for Jesuits' formation. Then he isolated the one quality that enables the four characteristics to bloom: "Loyola's Spiritual Exercises also instilled 'indifference,' freedom from attachments to places and possessions which could result in inappropriate resistance to movement or change."[6]

When you are no longer blinded by the plank in your eye, you become open to taking courageous action you would never have dared to take before. Matthew 7:5 enables you to see your life-size challenges through the eyes of God. In so doing, you will find the courage to act boldly yet humbly. Your soul becomes quenched with relief when you do what the Spirit has prompted in you.

I profoundly experienced this during my first divorce. Seventeen months, four court appearances, and tens of thousands of dollars in legal fees led to a thirty-eight-page separation agreement. In it, I was to receive about 16 percent of my infant son's time. I was deeply torn. I was afraid that this limited amount would result in me having at best a "visiting uncle" relationship with him. I wanted to be as complete a father as I could be. Yet, I was emotionally drained and desperately wanted to move on. Though I was not yet a committed believer, I felt an unusual and strong inner prompt: *Don't sign it!*

After much nerve-racking reflection and advice seeking, I took a leap of faith to pursue my only available alternative: to seek full custody myself. My lawyer warned the consequences were severe—two years in court, family members on the stand, and another $100,000 in legal fees. I decided that this was worth every dime I had. I was neutral about the money and about whether I won or lost. I simply knew what I needed to do and I felt at peace with my decision.

Four months and four more trips to court later, my unbudging ex-wife unexpectedly offered to settle. After a marathon nine-hour session with our two lawyers, I received 40 percent of my son's time and a fair financial support agreement. At that moment, I knew with unshakable certainty that God was real and that this unimaginable outcome was not of my own doing. I experienced a monthlong broken spirit—a profound and humbling awareness of God's love for me, an undeserving and sinful man. It was not my first, nor would it be the last. However, it was my deepest. When that month ended, I surrendered my life to Jesus and have never looked back.

Simone Weil spent her short life seeking to be close to God—to do his will as she best understood it. She came to know Jesus and became highly devoted to him, although she refused to formally join the Church. She feared that would bias her relationship with God. She has been called the greatest spiritual writer of the twentieth century.

Weil remained single and died at the age of thirty-four in England, in 1943. Friends created four books from her papers and letters that described her remarkable spiritual journey. Insightful passages from *Waiting for God* affirm from her experiences that we must be neutral and unattached to outcomes to be at peace with ourselves and with God.

She points out that resisting only brings us strife: "In struggling against anguish, one never produces serenity; the struggle against anguish only produces more anguish."[7] Only when we accept the reality of our situation will we find meaning in our anguish and see new options.

She makes a connection between a lack of attachments and the ability to be truthful:

> In this world, only those people who have fallen to the lowest degree of humiliation, far below beggary, who are not just without any social consideration but are regarded by all as being deprived of that foremost human dignity, reason itself—only those people, in fact, are capable of telling the truth. All the others lie.

When she says that all the others lie, she is saying that the rest of us have something to hide, prove, or lose. Our biases and attachments bind us and even blind us to being truthful. Being unattached frees us to be truthful, especially with ourselves. Perhaps we need to actually have nothing in order to be capable of telling the truth. I believe we only have to be *willing* to have nothing. However, we can never know until we experience real losses.

Weil zeroes in on a truth about what fills our minds: "Imagination and fiction make up more than three-quarters of real life." The noise in our minds is mostly made up of imaginary scenarios. It is the real experience of our minds, but not real in the sense of the world we live in. This massive mental clutter is made up of our judgments—the thoughts and feelings we use to justify ourselves, blame others, and rationalize what we do. Judgments are the plank in our eye and the noise in our brain, blocking out love.

She speaks of the power of being in the present: "The highest ecstasy is attention at its fullest." When we become neutral about outcomes, our mind becomes uncluttered and we are then capable of giving our full attention to the moment, of being "in the present." The attention of your mind, body, heart, and soul is entirely focused on now, the only time that is real. True attention is love, which is why so many people crave attention but can scarcely give it. Jesus said the greatest command is "You shall love the Lord your God with all your heart, and with all your soul, and with all your mind" (Matthew 22:37). We fulfill this command when we are present, when we are free from worried thoughts, troubled hearts, and a distant soul. To be present, with our full attention on now, is to be very close to God. In Proverbs, this truth is written as, "Be still and know that I am God" (Psalm 46:10). God is eternal, and so is the present moment. Indeed, now and eternity are the same.

Weil describes how being present, neutral, and at peace affects others: "Difficult as it is to listen to someone in affliction, it is just as difficult for him to know that compassion is listening to him." Giving our full attention to another is intense and life-changing. If the other person shies away from such attention, don't take it personally. You are stirring something hidden deep within when you listen without agreeing or disagreeing. This is a central skill in the field of personal coaching.

Two thousand years ago, Jesus brilliantly demonstrated being neutral when he said to the people about to stone a woman for having committed adultery, "Let him who is without sin among you be the first to throw a stone at her" (John 8:7). He was at peace whether they stoned her or not. In response, the condemners laid down their stones, freely and willingly.

The apostle Peter described how Jesus handled people who attacked him. "When he was reviled, he did not revile in return; when he suffered, he did not threaten; but he trusted to him who judges justly" (1 Peter 2:23). He lived his own words, turning the other cheek in humble obedience. Obedience is a hard but necessary lesson. Our pride and ego groan in despair at its sight.

An old friend, struggling with major personal difficulties, opined to me through gritted teeth, "I'm a stubborn man; that's just who I am."

I replied, "Well it doesn't seem to be working for you anymore. Perhaps you need to replace the word 'stubborn' with a new word."

"Oh," he replied. "What's that?"

I felt stirred from a deep place within and said, "Obedience." His face fell. He later told me that moment changed his life. For the first time in his life, he let God in.

Being neutral means being true to the Spirit within— free from fear-based self-protection—even if other people disapprove. The effect we then have on others will often surprise us. David is a friend who unconsciously used Matthew 7:5 when he was in Jamaica, traveling by taxi with a friend. They entered a small, impoverished town and through the open windows, he heard some teenagers on the street menacingly call out, "White dogs." At a stop sign, he noticed two black Jamaican men standing in front of a pretty post office building and took a picture. Immediately, one man scowled, saying, "How much are you going to pay me for that picture?" Caught off guard, David replied without thinking, "How much does the prime minister of Jamaica charge to have his picture taken?"

The man replied, "Nothing."

David replied, "Then I guess that's your answer." The man shrugged, smiled, and wished him a good day.

Afterward, David was aghast at his actions. First of all, he would have gladly paid the man a few dollars. Second, it wasn't his nature to be so bold. What if this man had become angry? But the Spirit had taken hold and put the right words in his mouth. Jesus assured his disciples, "But when they deliver you up, do not be anxious how you are to speak or what you are to say; for what you are to say will be given to you in that hour" (Matthew 10:19). When we are neutral, we can confidently and authentically speak what we think and feel right in the moment, without prescreening ourselves using Protector. We can trust God if we are neutral and unattached, ready to accept whatever happens next as his will. David's bold words unwittingly removed a speck from that man: the fault of extorting money from strangers.

To be that bold, you need to embrace one life-changing truth about yourself: You are worthy of being loved as you are now, in spite of your faults. But do you really want that depth of peace? Let's find out.

ELEVEN

Do You Want Results or Peace?

When we choose results first and peace second, we are rejecting God's peace. In the following story, a man explores what is robbing his peace through seeking to resolve an everyday household irritation that has bothered him for several years. In examining his experience, you may recognize your own patterns of resistance to awakening the bravest part of your inner self so that you can resolve everyday issues positively in the Spirit.

Kirk sat down heavily in the big chair nestled beside the fireplace. His cropped red hair showed wisps of gray, and a short beard covered his thick neck. He looked down at his heavy bulk and took a deep breath. "I get in a bad space sometimes," he said. "A couple of days ago, I was really bummed, almost depressed."

We had been friends sharing our Christian journey for two years, but only now was he opening up more personally. I caught his eye. "That sucks, man," I said sympathetically. "What do you think is bringing that on?"

He sighed. "Lots of things, I suppose. I'm working too late. I'm not getting enough sleep. I put back on thirty pounds I lost earlier this year. That part really bums me out. And I'm tired of having two grown sons living at home. Look at that pile of dirty pots over there!" A sizable stack of stainless steel dominated the sink in the open, partially renovated kitchen.

I focused on the pots, knowing deep spiritual truths lay hidden in the tiniest of issues. "What is it about the dirty pots that bothers you?"

Surprisingly, he answered me directly. "Well, Daniel likes to cook but he doesn't like to clean up after himself. So I end up doing it and it pisses me off, frankly!" Daniel was Kirk's older son, twenty-nine years old and going back to school in search of a career that had so far eluded him. "Sometimes I can't believe my wife and I still have both our boys living at home. They're supposed to be living on their own by now."

"Why are they still living at home?" I asked.

"Well, when Daniel was twenty-one, he started hanging out with a bunch of guys who were into heavy drinking, and we got worried about him living on his own. So we had him come home just to keep him away from that gang. We thought that would get him back on track, but now it's been eight years and he's still here!"

I decided to be bold. "Kirk, the solution to all of your troubles can be found in that pile of dirty pots."

He let out a skeptical laugh. "Yeah, sure!"

"I mean it," I said. "The reason that pile of dirty pots bothers you is the same reason that your boys are still living at home and the same reason you wake up bummed, tired, and overworked."

"Oh, you mean this Peace Promise thing that you wrote."

"That's right."

"I read that draft of your book you sent a few months ago, and I still don't really understand the idea of getting neutral and having a plank in my eye."

I dug deeper. "Well, let's use the pile of pots as an example. Do you have a biased point of view about that pile?"

Kirk was taken aback. "Look, there's nothing bad about wanting a clean kitchen!"

"I didn't ask if your point of view was bad. I only asked if it was biased."

"Well," he mused, "I suppose it is. I want the dishes done and I want Daniel to do the work, not me."

"I agree. You want a certain result and you want to get that result in a certain way—that is, to have Daniel clean up after himself. You're not neutral about it."

"Well, so what? I mean, it's just good parenting to want your kids to do the right thing."

"Of course," I replied. "But are you neutral about it?"

"No, I'm not neutral, and why should I be?"

"Only if you want to include God in solving your problem. When you have a biased point of view, it means you are solving your problem alone, on your own strength." I knew Kirk would relate to this foundational Scripture, in which Jesus said that we can do nothing apart from him (John 15:5).

"Look, if you think you see a way I can get Daniel to do the dishes, why don't you just tell me? As a businessperson, I'll pay someone to give me results."

I replied, "There are probably ten ways to get Daniel to do the dishes. Any one of them could work. What I don't know is which one will work for you. All I can tell you is that if you first get neutral about the result you want, you will see clearly which one is right for you."

"So you're saying that's all you will do—help me get 'neutral.' You won't actually help me solve my problem." He sounded mildly exasperated.

"That's right. If you learn how to remove the plank from your eye, then you will know how to solve the dirty pot problem with Daniel and how to get your work done sooner, get more sleep, and get out of feeling depressed."

Kirk considered my words for a moment. "Look, I always thought that teaching from Jesus meant I had a universal plank—that I have one big plank blinding me."

"That's not my experience. We have a plank in our eye about each individual thing that bothers us. That means we have hundreds of them, and we have to dig them out one at a time. It might sound overwhelming but if you do it each time something irritates you, you solve that problem *and* you shrink the pile!" I chuckled to myself at the image of the stack of planks I'd pulled out over the years.

"Oh." Kirk was pensive, digesting the picture.

"Do you want to try it right now, Kirk?" I asked.

"OK."

"All right. What is it about that pile of dirty pots that bothers you?"

He hesitated before spitting it out. "I'm already swamped. I come in here and I just go, 'Arghh!' It's one more thing to do. Maybe I'm just too lazy to clean them up myself."

"Maybe. Personally, I believe that lazy is a label and labels always sit on top of the real reason."

"I don't know about that," Kirk retorted. "Sloth is one of the seven deadly sins."

"Perhaps, but there's always a reason we choose to do what we do. It's like the old Chinese saying: 'Ask why seven times and you shall know the truth.'" I shifted gears. "Kirk, let me ask you one more question."

"All right, ask away."

"Why do you think you're being lazy about not cleaning up the pots?"

"It's probably because I think that it wasn't me who made the mess, so why should I have to clean it up."

"Is that a neutral point of view?"

"No. It's the one I want to have. I want Daniel to clean up his own mess."

"How long have you been trying to get Daniel to do that?"

"Since forever." He laughed. "I know, I know. The definition of insanity is to keep doing the same thing hoping you'll get a different result!"

I chuckled. "Exactly! The plank in your eye is why you're not seeing what you need to do to be successful. You've been failing to get the result you want for eight years."

"So how do I get neutral?"

"Well, the full answer has many layers to it, but the simple answer is to accept the possibility that he'll never clean up the dishes."

"Well, that's too much to ask," he said bluntly.

"What do you mean?" I asked, curious about his reasoning.

"I mean it's hard for me to go all the way to accepting the thing that I don't want. I think that what this is making me do is realize that I need to stop. It's like a big red sign that says, 'Stop. First get neutral.' That way I prevent

myself from getting angry or saying something I'll regret."
He explained himself further, somewhat sheepishly. "I'm
the kind of guy who needs a process. You know, like step
one, step two, step three . . ."

"That's a cool idea, Kirk. You need to stop first, for sure.
So if this teaching does that, it's already helped you a lot.
Still, you only open yourself to the Spirit if you go all the
way. Otherwise, you are still choosing to do what you're
doing based on your own thoughts and feelings about
what seems right to you. My experience with using Jesus'
teaching on this is that as long as I am not neutral about a
matter that is troubling me, I cannot trust myself to make
the right decision. My biases will slant my actions and
others will see and feel that. This causes them to react,
usually negatively, to whatever I do."

"So I have to go the whole way." Kirk furrowed his brow.

"Yes." He sat quietly. I prompted him. "You look like this
is bad news."

"Well, it's not bad news. It's just more than I wanted or
hoped I would have to do. I'd really just like the answer on
how to get Daniel to do the dishes and be done with it!"
This was Kirk the businessman speaking—give me results!

I persisted. "Look, when you do it Jesus' way, you will
know how to solve this problem and your other problems.
Not necessarily the way you want to do it, but the way
God wants you to play your role."

"So let's say I'm neutral now," he shot back.

"Ah, now you're just playing with me," I said with a grin.

"No, I mean it. I'm neutral," he insisted.

"Getting neutral is not an academic exercise. You'll only know for sure when the thing that bothers you happens again and you're at peace with it."

"Seriously, I accept that I could be doing Daniel's dishes forever. For real."

"Then you will see clearly what you need to do."

"That's it?"

"Look, I can give you a page of thirty tips for influencing other people to change willingly. But if you're not neutral first, these are just ways to manipulate people. When you get neutral, you let go of your attachment to your idea of the 'right answer.' That frees you to choose what you do wisely and to be at peace if you don't get the result you hoped for. It works that way because you've invited God to participate in solving the problem. You do your part and he does his. This makes it sacred."

"Yes, I see that. It's like making a God-centric decision instead of a human-centric one." Kirk was a quick study.

I stood up and gave the big man a bear hug. "This was good for me," he said sincerely as I left.

I share Kirk's experience with you for one reason. We are all like Kirk. We don't want peace first. We want results first. Kirk wanted clean dishes first and only then would he be at peace with his son's irritating habit. This is the stubborn human way that keeps us trapped in unhappiness over troubling issues for years. When we choose Jesus' way, we often see startling new ways to get what we want when we are at peace with not getting it in the first place. Matthew 7:5 is a mind-blowing paradox in which we become spiritually powerful only after we become humanly powerless.

You have a stark choice: Do you want peace more than the outcomes that matter to you? More than avoiding conflict? More than a certain lifestyle? More than your favorite addictions and indulgences? More than clinging to a job for the paycheck? More than seeing your child succeed by your definition? Even more than daydreaming and fantasizing? These hopes and worries steal your peace. Your only escape is to intentionally release them, sometimes as life forces it on you and sometimes as a free-will choice.

TWELVE

You Are Lovable

Your life changes when you are aligned with God's will for you. Your purpose is clear—to love and be loved in the here and now. Your confidence is solid; you know you can do his will and accept the unpleasant parts that go with it. You accept that suffering is necessary and temporary. The delusions of the ego are being torn away, separating flesh from spirit. "For the desires of the flesh are against the Spirit, and the desires of the Spirit are against the flesh; for these are opposed to each other, to prevent you from doing what you would" (Galatians 5:17).

No one is doing it to you. You are causing your own anxiety and unhappiness when you fail to trust God and try to control things that are not yours to control. Like a barometer, peace is the ever-present measure of your inner state of being.

Underneath your unhappiness lies a core question: Are you lovable as you are now, specks and all? Not being loved for who we are is a deep-seated fear for most of us. On the one hand, we are afraid we are being used. On the other hand, we are afraid that if someone really knew the darkest corners of our thoughts, he or she would run for the hills.

When I was young, I was convinced that if I made enough money, people would like me and want to hang out with me. I made a secret bargain with "life" that if I got rich, I would give a lot of the money away. I would be a good guy with the money, not like those other greedy rich guys. It is a Faustian fantasy I have heard others admit to. My motive was simple: I wanted to be liked, comfortable, and, yes, envied. I didn't believe I was lovable in my own right. I craved the attention and admiration that money would bring.

When I began dating as a young man, I was secretly afraid women who liked me were not interested in the real me. I feared they were interested in my earning capacity. When I later married, that changed. I then suspected she saw me as a possession, something she needed to complete her self-image and impress the people who mattered to her. No woman could want me just for me. Like Groucho Marx famously declared, I didn't care to join any club that would have me as a member!

Inevitably, we test people, especially our mates. Do they really love us? A husband thinks, "Hmm, I wonder how she will react if I leer at that woman walking by in the bikini." A wife thinks, "I wonder what he'll say if I drop $500 on a new dress without talking to him first." A rebellious teen does the opposite of her parents' wishes to prove her independence. She feels their desire for her success as pressure to please them, not respect for her own dreams.

What are we doing? We are finding each other's buttons. We are discovering what is safe and what is not. We are deciding what we can be real about and what we need to hide. We want to know if people who matter to us love even the dark side of our personalities. What we are actually doing is testing whether we are existentially lovable. This is normal, except for when the tests seem too intense to bear. Then the relationship tears at the seams of its fabric. Fighting escalates and emotional distance builds cold, loveless walls.

"That which you fear you cause to occur" is a mantra that encourages me to face these love tests. It is paradoxical that if we want to experience serenity and inner peace, we must look squarely at our deepest fears. The Peace Promise drags us kicking and screaming toward conquering them. We cry out, "If you really loved me, you would change for me!" Pain leads to judgments that cause heated words. Love evaporates like vapor in the wind. Our partner's refusal to meet our needs pierces us with the terrifying possibility that we are not lovable as we are now. Otherwise we think, "Why would you so cruelly withhold love from me, especially after all I have poured into this relationship?"

My battle with my first wife over access to our child was God's means of bringing this truth home to me. During this two-year period, I became aware of a vision of a cold chunk of ice locked deep within me. Frozen inside were my emotions, firmly locked away in fear of their uncontrollable explosiveness. Looking at my fears shone God's light on my inner being. Quaking and shivering, surrounded by a loving support network, and grounded in my nascent faith, I embraced my fear of my feelings— sometimes via a punching bag workout, sometimes through therapy and coaching, and always grounded in real-life events.

As my chunk of ice melted over a period of months, I began to see in my mind's eye a small green pea glistening in the middle. I became able to feel that pea, just as the fabled princess could feel the pea buried under twenty mattresses. I suffered humbling defeats and became ever more vulnerable. As I did, God's blessing and his love appeared without fail. I knew then that he loved me in spite of my faults. With repeated experiences, I learned that all my struggles led me to the same destination: the reward of his peace and the wisdom to know what to do—but only after a full surrender with no escape routes and nothing held back.

Debbie discovered this startling truth for herself. Her husband had left her and their four young children for another woman. He provided child support and saw the children regularly, but five years later, she was left feeling alone and unhappy, even while clinging to her Christian faith. Despite her aloneness, she resisted dating other men. With my coaching help, she used Matthew 7:5 and was able to see with sudden clarity in just one hour why she was keeping the dating door closed: She felt embarrassed by visible scars that were the result of cosmetic breast surgery four years earlier. She feared that a man would be repulsed by the sight of her scars. By exploring her beliefs with me as if she had nothing to hide, she suddenly accepted that if a man would reject her for that reason, she would not want him anyway. Her heart instantly opened. One month later, she met the man who would soon become her new husband.

Was it a coincidence? I don't believe so. God reveals his presence when we get neutral about the outcome we fear the most. I have come to believe that if the worst thing actually does happen, something good will come out of it, something I could never have imagined. His plan is wiser than our plan. We discover his love for us by separating our self-worth from the events that happen to us in life.

Another client struggled greatly with his beliefs about getting married. He and his girlfriend had been together for seven years and were approaching their midthirties. Conscious of her own ticking biological clock, she was pressuring him to make a full commitment. He and I explored the first layer of the plank in his eye: his beliefs. He feared the public nature of making a commitment. He was afraid of what others would think if he failed in his marriage. He recognized the link between marriage and having children. This also triggered fears about change and having control of his lifestyle. One week later, he announced to me with great joy, "I asked her to marry me!" Merely naming his fears caused them to melt away. God's light shone on the darkness of his long-held beliefs. He became neutral about the negative outcomes and instantly, a lifelong blessing blossomed for both of them.

It took me seventeen years to reach a point where I truly felt at peace with the difficulties in my life. Once we experience the closeness to God that comes with being neutral, unbiased, unattached, and surrendered, we feel his constant love in the here and now. Yesterday's peace is gone. Tomorrow's peace is unknown. We must want his peace more than anything else, right now.

Christian social activist Dorothy Day understood what it took to feel close to God. She said, "I really only love

God as much as I love the person I love the least." Even one resentful grudge separates us from God's love and prevents us from seeing people with the eyes of Jesus. We think we are protecting ourselves from getting hurt but we are in fact blocking out love, leaving ourselves frustrated, unhappy, and unsuccessful at positively impacting others, people with whom we live and work and whom we care for a great deal. We are in fact not being spiritually sensible.

When we first get neutral about outcomes to which we are strongly attached, we break free and become secure in who we are. We become true to the person we were born to be, without trying to extract love from others. St. Paul wrote, "If I give away all I have, and if I deliver my body to be burned, but have not love, I gain nothing" (1 Corinthians 13:3).

When we have love, we have everything. We are lovable. We become a love disturber for others, rattling them with our being and awakening their innate desire to love and be loved. But our ego must pay a price: "For if any one thinks he is something, when he is nothing, he deceives himself" (Galatians 6:3).

We must embrace our nothingness, doing the opposite of what our ego craves and cries out for. We are pawns in an eternal chess match. Humbly doing our part gives us his peace and love, now and forever. Then we are able to resolve troubling issues clearly, calmly, and confidently.

Jesus proves this to us beyond a doubt by delivering results we know we did not cause to happen.

The apostle Paul put our earthly life into perspective beautifully in 1 Corinthians 13:12–13: "Now we see in a mirror dimly; but then face to face. Now I know in part; then I shall understand fully, even as I have been fully understood. So faith, hope, love abide, these three; but the greatest of these is love."

The Peace Promise teaches us the meaning of true spiritual love. In the present moment, we can know only in part. But in Jesus, we have faith and hope in our future that God will make all things right according to his will. Thus we can receive his peace today, not as the world gives but as Jesus gives. Our hearts shall not be troubled and we shall not be afraid.

TAKE IT FURTHER

COURSES

KuypersLeadership.com is a learning organization for people who want to first seek his peace in order to resolve troubling situations. You will find information on e-courses, live events, and other books.

BOOKS

John Kuypers' earlier books provide readers in-depth learning on each of the three stages of the spiritual journey toward peace. This is the recommended order of reading:

- *What's Important Now* (2002), John's top seller, is about being authentic with nothing to hide, by shedding the past so you can live in the present. Available in print and as an e-book.

- *The Non-Judgmental Christian* (2004) is John's provocative e-book about how three nothings will transform your most important relationships. You soften your heart by learning to live as if you have nothing to prove.

- *Who's the Driver Anyway?* (2011) is John's collaborative leadership book on resolving difficult issues at work by agreeing on shared authority and who gets to decide. Available in hard cover at http://carswell.com and on Amazon Kindle worldwide except in Canada.

- *Comfortable in Your Own Skin* (2006) is a short, inspirational e-book that captures twelve principles for living in the present as revealed in ninety-nine inspired moments.

- "Near and Far" is a short e-booklet that helps couples heal deep unhappiness and power struggles caused by having opposite ways of resolving conflict. You find your very soul by learning to live as if you have nothing to lose.

BLOG POSTS

Subscribe to John's blog at http://johnkuypers.com for more than 130 posts that help you find peace in common troubling issues on your spiritual journey.

SOCIAL MEDIA

YouTube: http://youtube.com/johngkuypers
Twitter: Follow John at http://twitter.com/johnkuypers.

Facebook: Get regular posts at http://facebook.com/
johnkuyperspage.

ABOUT THE AUTHOR

John Kuypers is an author, business executive, leadership coach, and speaker. Following a stress-related blackout in his mid-thirties, John began a personal journey to overcome the causes of his carefully hidden unhappiness and anxiety. This journey led him back to his Catholic faith, and he now teaches others how to live in the present, resolve their relationship difficulties, and experience new levels of peace and wholeness.

http://johnkuypers.com

NOTES

1. Paul Tillich, *The Courage to Be* (New Haven, Conn.: Yale University Press, 1952).

2. Mihaly Csikszentmihalyi, *Flow: The Psychology of Optimal Experience* (New York: Harper & Row, 1990).

3. Anne Graham Lotz, *Wounded by God's People: Discovering How God's Love Heals Our Hearts* (Grand Rapids, Mich.: Zondervan, 2013).

4. Ibid.

5. Eugene O'Kelly, *Chasing Daylight: How My Forthcoming Death Transformed My Life* (New York: McGraw-Hill Education, 2007), p. 6.

6. Chris Lowney, *Heroic Leadership: Best Practices from a 450-Year-Old Company That Changed the World* (Chicago: Loyola Press, 2005), chapter two.

7. Simone Weil, *Waiting for God* (New York: Harper Perennial, 2009).